The Manned Planetary Space Vehicle conceived by Boeing, and based upon its 1968 Mars Mission Study, leaves Earth in five stages. This is the ignition sequence, or second stage, with the first stage returning to low Earth orbit.

THOMAS W. BECKER

EXPLORING TOMORROW
SPACE

Introduction by
WERNHER von BRAUN

STERLING PUBLISHING CO., INC.
NEW YORK

OTHER BOOKS OF INTEREST

Atomic Light: Lasers—What They Are and How They Work
Breeding Laboratory Animals
Complete Science Course for Young Experimenters

Marvels of Medical Engineering
Microscope — and How to Use It
Physics Through Experiment

Riches of the Sea

Basic Biology in Color:
Vol. 1: Animal Kingdom   Vol. 3: Human Biology
Vol. 2: Plant World   Vol. 4: Human Reproductive System
Vol. 5: Ecology

Acknowledgments

The author is greatly indebted to various officials of the National Aeronautics and Space Administration, especially those in Washington D.C., for taking the time to review the entire manuscript to assure its accuracy. Les Gaver, Chief of the Audio Visual Branch of the Public Affairs Office, deserves a special word of thanks for helping obtain nearly all the photographs for the book and for helping coordinate some of the research and review. They do wish me to point out, however, that while everything discussed here is certainly within the realm of possibility, NASA itself does not have a complete budget for all of the planned activities.

Manufactured in the United States of America
All rights reserved
Library of Congress Catalog Card No.: 72–81033
ISBN 0-8069-3048-9   UK 7061 2392-1
3049-7

CONTENTS

Three different configurations of orbiting astronomical observatories are shown in this artist's concept, all based on the use of solar cell panels for electrical supply.

A hypothetical four-stage, chemical-rocket-propelled space vehicle for interplanetary travel as it might appear on a round trip between Earth and Mars satellite orbits. Large pods at lower right contain quarters for an eight-man crew. The craft is an orbiter and, while it is not designed to land on a planet's surface, the upper structure, with its chemical rockets, is detachable and could make a soft landing on Mars.

INTRODUCTION

In exploring space, we are indeed exploring man's tomorrow. Our movement into space in the past dozen years can be likened to the first tentative crossings of the Bering Strait by nomads into the New World, thereby opening a whole new future for the race of man.

The initial lunar explorations, the probing of our solar system by scientific spacecraft, and the gathering of great quantities of data on extraterrestrial phenomena, are much more significant achievements than a mark of man's technological cleverness. The first manned landing on the Moon is not just another milestone in human history. It signaled the opening of a new era of human development even more profound than the crossing of the Bering Strait.

The clear meaning of our space flight capabilities is that man no longer is bound to his home planet.

Man has *left* Earth. Search as we will in history and pre-history, no comparable statement of such fateful import can be found until, written in the rocks of Olduvai Gorge in east Africa, we read, Man *appeared* on Earth, a million or more years ago.

But there is one very significant difference between these two events. By setting foot on another world, man did so by conscious design and effort. His appearance on Earth, however, was not by his plan, and such effort as he put into making an appearance at all was directed almost entirely by an instinct for survival.

A moral implication fairly shouts for recognition in these two contrasting major events of human existence. In the one, no conscious choice was made, no resolve to take the road to humanity was formed. But, in choosing to explore space, man, for the first time, has assumed responsibility for what may well prove to be a radical turn in human evolution. The mere fact that we have this capability of choice points to a higher destiny.

The venture into space is the first step into a novel environment. It is wholly alien, even contrary, to the earthly conditions to which we have slowly adapted over eons of time.

Can man now, over the ensuing ages, adapt to conditions of extra-terrestrial existence? Can he even survive a significant period of time away from his Mother Earth?

The obstacles against extending the human ecological range outside Earth are enormous. But, insuperable? Man's imaginative ingenuity and persistence will overcome them.

Indeed, we have already begun to do so. There is a new future out there.

—WERNHER VON BRAUN

How the Moon's floor looked to a lunar orbiter in 1966. This photograph was transmitted from the spacecraft to a monitoring station in California. The same probing method will be followed in the exploring of Mars, Jupiter and other planets, according to present plans.

Foreword

As a young boy, I grew up on a diet of Buck Rogers, Flash Gordon and the magnificent space art paintings of Chesley Bonestell. On many occasions, I tried to put myself to sleep while the spoken words of Willy Ley and Donald Menzel were still ringing in my ears. I believed then, as I still do, that I was born too soon and would live out my life without ever seeing astronauts speed off into space. My college classes in astronomy were sheer adventure and probably as much as anything helped shape my thinking about the enormous potential of exploring space.

Since then, I have been particularly fortunate (as many of us have) to be able to watch "man leave the cradle of the Earth" as the Soviet pioneer Konstantin Tsiolkovsky so aptly put it, and crawl in agonizingly small footsteps up to the Moon. Having been a witness to these exciting events, and to some of the actual Apollo launches, I am confident that much of what is written in this book will come to pass.

What is contained in these pages is scientific fact, and is as reasonable an explanation of what we can expect in space in the future as can be found anywhere. The exploration of space is an inspiring epic of truly heroic proportion, and those who pursue it are daily earning our sincerest admiration. A great portion of the world population, though, is not sufficiently informed about space and our assault on it to appreciate what is being done. The book is addressed to both audiences in the hope it will give further support to the first and renewed courage to the second.

It is difficult to write any kind of book today on astronomy or space because our knowledge is expanding at such a rapid rate that changes occur almost overnight. For these reasons, some of the concepts and projects explained here will change, some greatly and others to a lesser degree, some perhaps even while the book is being produced. Scheduling of new programs depends mainly upon the availability of funds to set plans in motion. The pursuit of knowledge in space can be speeded up or slowed down, but hopefully it will not cease altogether now that it has begun.

Exploring Tomorrow in Space draws upon work being done by space agencies around the world, especially the National Aeronautics and Space Administration. Although the shapes of vehicles, travel times, dates of projected events and the appearances of different objects may all change, the fundamental principles underlying them still remain the same. Our capabilities in space depend upon discovering new scientific truths and learning how to use them. Once learned, they can be applied anywhere. This is one of the most important concepts learned in what has come to be known as "space science."

This book has two purposes: to explain the many complexities of the space environment, and to help interpret generally our methods of dealing with them. If these two purposes are served, new generations will find a more meaningful place in their lives for space exploration.

Almost every object in this photograph is a galaxy—each faint spot and streak of light represents a complete system of very many hundreds of millions of stars. Only the bright round objects with "spikes" are stars in our own system—everything else is so distant that the light which made this picture was several hundred million years on its journey. This is not a photograph as things *are*. But as they were—many scores of millions of years before man appeared on Earth.

1. PUTTING THE MOON TO WORK

Man's first steps on the Moon in July, 1969, were the final result of many years of hard work and the constant search for scientific solutions to physical problems. Hundreds of thousands of aerospace technicians, millions of man-hours of thought and work, thousands of conferences, all merged together during the period 1958–1969 to finally place two men on the lunar surface and return them safely to Earth. That this achievement is one of the truly great accomplishments of civilized man is obvious, but even more important is the fact that it was done with a minimum of error. This is a stirring tribute to the ability of "thinking man" to overcome problems, to find answers, and to benefit from new knowledge. The whole program was developed in the United States under the National Aeronautics and Space Administration (NASA) whose plans for the future constitute a large part of this book.

Reaching the Moon was accomplished in four main stages. Each stage had highly significant implications for man's future survival and exploration in space:

STAGE 1: (PROJECT MERCURY)

An experiment to test a vehicle and various on-board systems to determine if a man could survive flight in space. Six Mercury spacecraft were tested carefully and successfully, each carrying a single astronaut, from 1961 through 1964.

STAGE 2: (PROJECT GEMINI)

An experiment to determine if it was possible for separate spacecraft to meet in space (rendezvous), come together and dock, and to determine if man could survive long periods of time in space. Ten Gemini spacecraft were orbited around Earth, each carrying two astronauts, from 1965 through 1966. Several astronauts floated freely in space.

STAGE 3: (PROJECT APOLLO)

An experiment to test a three-man vehicle capable of going to the Moon, landing on the lunar surface, and returning safely to Earth. Ten Apollo spacecraft were successfully tested; five of them landed on the Moon and returned to lunar orbit to dock with the Apollo Command Module. The program, begun with Apollo 7 in 1968, concluded with Apollo 17 in 1972.

STAGE 4: (PROJECTS RANGER, SURVEYOR, ORBITER)

A concentrated program of photographic investigation of the Moon to determine its major features, study its terrain, select possible spacecraft landing sites, and measure its geological composition to learn if it could support the weight of a landed spacecraft.

These four stages were virtually completed by the end of July, 1969—just $8\frac{1}{2}$ years after the launch of the first Mercury spacecraft—in one of the most inspiring decades of creative scientific technology. The amount of information obtained during that time is so immense it will take many years to fully understand precisely what it all means.

The spacecraft that were designed to carry out these four stages represent the same basic designs from which succeeding vehicles have been and will be built. For example, the Ranger spacecraft was modified slightly to become the Mariner spacecraft which investigated Venus and Mars. The Apollo three-man spacecraft is now being altered in case a vehicle is needed to land a team of three men on Mars in the 1980's. Both the Surveyor and Orbiter spacecraft have been modified for use in photographing the other planets in our Solar System.

With increasing success and confidence in their technology, men will be moving in space farther and farther away from the Earth, as the rest of this book will show. The next several decades in space may establish manned stations in orbit of Earth and Moon, may allow men to build and maintain Moon bases and large whole colonies, may investigate Mars and Venus more closely, and may finally land a manned expedition on the Martian landscape. Beyond this, we now envision a day when astro-missions continually ferry men and supplies back and forth between Mars, Earth, and our Moon, while at the same time men begin to explore and colonize the outer planets of our Solar System.

What we shall learn from our own Solar System is impossible to guess, but we already have enough of a view of space exploration to believe that the new knowledge coming from the stars and other planets will forge an entirely new concept of life as we know it now. This quest for new ideas and new knowledge will certainly challenge our best minds and capabilities, and put man to the ultimate test of his endurance and courage.

The Skylab Project

If men are to use space to advantage, they must learn how to live there. They must learn how to function usefully in the space environment in order to carry out research, maintain orbiting vehicles, provide stopping places for men en route between planets, and accomplish all the little odd jobs necessary to expand capabilities in space. The first step toward this goal is called *Project*

An artist's sketch depicts an orbiting Skylab "cluster" with solar cell panels extended out from the telescope mount in a paddle or windmill configuration. An Apollo Command and Service Module (CSM) is docked with it at the left.

Skylab, an orbiting space workshop equivalent to a five-room house high above the Earth.

Skylab looks like a large vacuum bottle. Weighing some 39 tons, it is composed of four different important parts. The main workshop cylinder is 48 feet long and has a diameter of about $21\frac{1}{2}$ feet. It is actually the third stage of the giant Saturn V rocket, called the S-IVB stage, that was used to boost Apollo spacecraft toward the Moon. Ordinarily the S-IVB stage carries fuel, but through ingenious planning it has been renovated and made into a living chamber complete with bedroom, kitchen, bathroom and a combination laboratory-workshop.

A large protrusion at one end of the cylinder houses the airlock-connecting tunnel. At the end of the airlock, outside, is a docking mechanism which will allow an Apollo spacecraft to dock with Skylab so the crew can transfer from the Apollo Command Module to the workshop, crawling first through the docking tunnel and then through the airlock to emerge into the workshop. The first three-man crew in Skylab will spend 28 days there. A second three-man crew is to replace the first and remain in the station for 56 days, some-

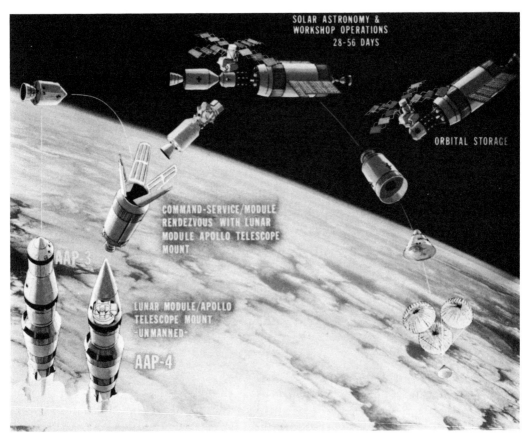

The planned sequence of the Apollo Application Program (AAP) to launch a telescope in space will be: 1—The orbital storage Workshop containing food among other things, is deployed into orbit of about 250 miles. 2—A manned re-supply Command and Service Module (CSM) is launched. 3—The Lunar Module/Apollo Telescope Mount (LM/ATM) is launched. 4—The CSM rendezvous with the LM/ATM takes place, and they join the Workshop. 5—The crew returns in the CSM.

time in 1973. A third replacement crew, scheduled also in 1973, is to live and work in the workshop for eight weeks.

Skylab is a true space station. It is expected to orbit the Earth continually at a fixed distance of 242 miles and a fixed rate of speed, which can be changed by the crew by using little positioning rockets. The rockets keep the station from wandering out of its intended orbit. From the sides of the large cylinder, two solar cell array panels will extend to convert sunlight into electricity to power the station. Electricity will operate such appliances as lights, water containers, communications equipment and research instruments.

Also attached to Skylab, and projecting out at a right angle to the main cylinder, is a specially designed Apollo Telescope Mount (ATM), a solar telescope whose mirror photographs the crew will use to study the Sun.

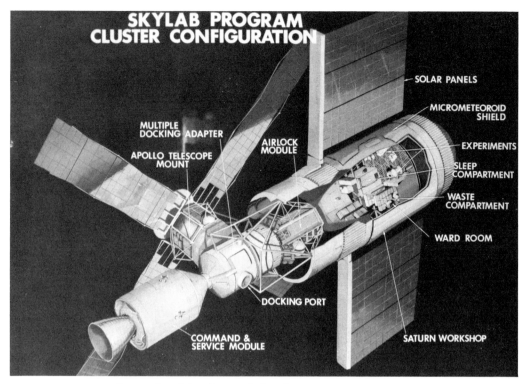

An underside view of the Skylab configuration.

Stretching outward from the telescope mount are four large "paddles" or arms—panels of solar cells to give separate electrical power to the telescope/observatory section of Skylab. The long panel arms give the ATM a strange "windmill" appearance.

Skylab crews will have many duties to perform. Once free of the Earth's atmosphere which diffuses light coming to Earth-based equipment when studying the heavens, Skylab's position in space will permit man's first accurate telescopic observation of the Sun. The astronauts are expected to experience many new discoveries because of the clearness with which they can see out into space. The Skylab telescope will be able to "see" 100 times more effectively than the Mount Wilson Observatory 200-inch telescope—the finest piece of telescopic equipment on Earth. It may locate more stars than we believed existed, stars formerly obscured by the Earth's atmosphere.

Scientists who specialize in studying the Sun and solar phenomena have been unable to study the universe in all its wavelengths. Without the blunting and filtering effect of an atmosphere, astronomers on Skylab will be able to study in the infrared, X-ray, gamma ray and radio wavelengths. They will be able to photograph the Sun during certain solar phenomena, and to study sunspots.

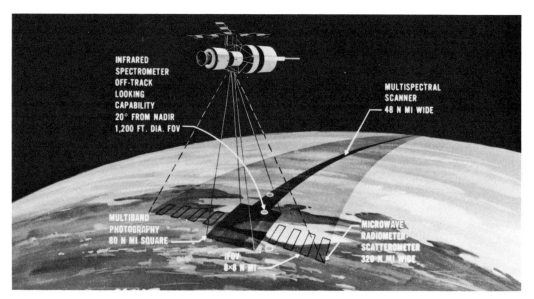

Skylab will investigate selected portions of the Earth with special photographic equipment. The Skylab Earth-Survey program will assist in developing new agricultural concepts, too, with infrared photography, which reveals how various crops are thriving. (See color picture on page H.)

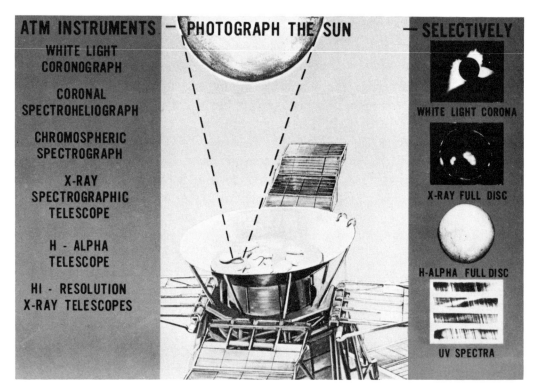

Instruments in the Skylab Apollo Telescope Mount (ATM) program can conduct a surprisingly broad variety of experiments in the investigation of the Sun, using ultraviolet (UV) light and X-ray telescopes, among other things.

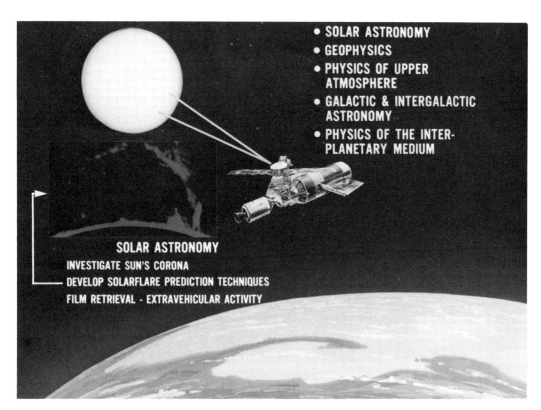

- SOLAR ASTRONOMY
- GEOPHYSICS
- PHYSICS OF UPPER ATMOSPHERE
- GALACTIC & INTERGALACTIC ASTRONOMY
- PHYSICS OF THE INTER-PLANETARY MEDIUM

SOLAR ASTRONOMY
INVESTIGATE SUN'S CORONA
DEVELOP SOLARFLARE PREDICTION TECHNIQUES
FILM RETRIEVAL - EXTRAVEHICULAR ACTIVITY

The post-Apollo Applications Program, of which Skylab is a part, will make use of the capabilities and discoveries developed in the Apollo Program to carry out continued scientific investigations from Earth orbit, such as shown here.

The Apollo Command and Service Module (CSM), used so successfully during the series of Apollo flights to the Moon, will be the prime crew-carrying craft for the Skylab project. It will dock with the ''cluster'' as shown in this diagram.

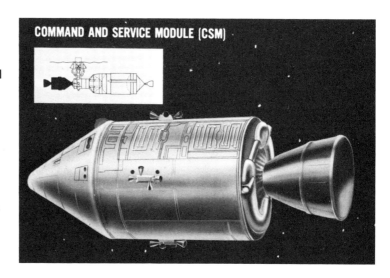

COMMAND AND SERVICE MODULE (CSM)

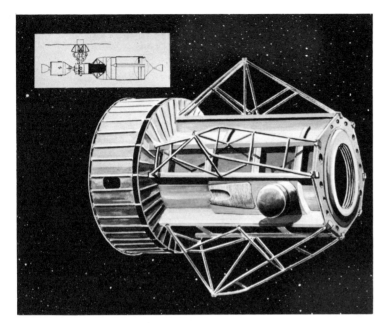

The Airlock Module acts as a safety compartment between the shirt-sleeve environment of the living and working areas of Skylab and the natural space environment. It also doubles in duty as an engine room for the cluster. It measures about 17 feet long, 10 feet in diameter, and weighs 9,000 pounds.

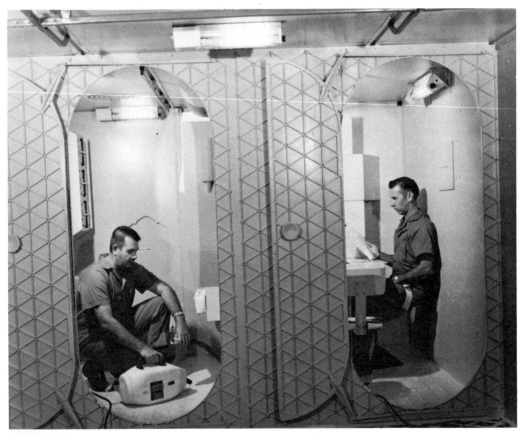

Skylab test engineers check out the craft's waste management (left) and food management sections in a full-scale mock-up session at NASA's Marshall Space Flight Center, Alabama.

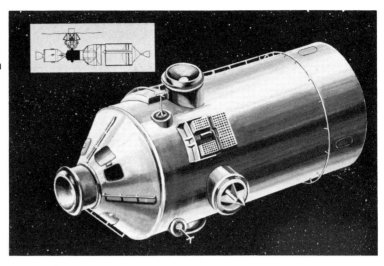

Skylab's Multiple Docking Adapter can receive as many as five Command and Service Modules at one time. It also serves as an in-orbit storage area. Weighing about 8,000 pounds, it measures 17 feet long and 10 feet in diameter.

Some of the most important research to be done from Skylab involves medical and biological sciences, especially studies of the effects of prolonged space living on the astronaut crews. Scientists want to know what happens to human functions in response to long periods of weightlessness, what the

(Left) Three test engineers, simulating the flight crew of Skylab, prepare a meal in the craft's wardroom section during mock exercises. (Right) Test engineers conduct biomedical experiments in the Skylab work compartment, showing how the lower body negative pressure device, a type of decompression chamber (lower left), operates and (right) how an exerciser called a metabolic activity ergometer works. These experiments are vitally important in learning how man can inhabit a permanent platform in space.

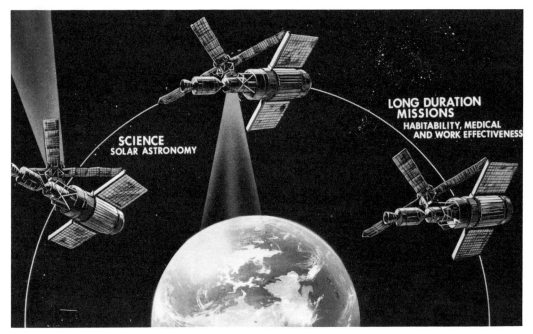

An artist's rendering explains the primary missions of Skylab.

psychological results are of a lack of the day-night cycle, of having to live in cramped quarters, or the response to the frustrations of a weightless environment.

Industrialists are eager to learn if the gravity-free space station can become a "space factory" where the lack of gravity can be an aid in the manufacture of lenses, bearings, electronic devices and perhaps even certain vaccines. New illness treatments could conceivably be found.

There are still other areas of study for the Skylab crews; mapping the Earth more precisely and inspecting specific agricultural and forest areas; detecting air and water pollution; charting the distribution of fish and studying the flow of certain ocean streams; following the movements of glaciers and icebergs; studying storm centers and different kinds of storms and cloud formations. Much of the crews' work will involve our own planet Earth.

During the first decade of manned space flight, emphasis was placed upon the physical fitness capabilities of the astronauts, a logical approach to dangerous and possibly permanently damaging expeditions into space. The primary astronaut of the future, however, will be a scientific specialist whose knowledge of science will be an outstanding qualification for missions in space. This does not mean these scientists will not have to be healthy; far from it. It does mean, however, that physical fitness will no longer be the prime consideration. Conceivably the time will arrive when engineers, photographers, professional economists, writers, and people from many other walks of life will be permitted in space.

Detailed examination of the many experiments planned to be carried out by Skylab crews during 1972 and 1973 reveals the incredible number of 51 major studies. Some of these studies are: (the parentheses enclose program designations) Extreme Ultraviolet Solar Coronal Spectroheliographs (S055A), Galactic X-ray Mapping (S150), Circadian Rhythm in the Vinegar Gnat (S072), Foot-Controlled Manoeuvring Unit (T020), Inflight Lower Body Negative Pressure (M092), Coronagraph Contamination Measurement (T025), Cytogenetic Studies of Blood (M111), Multispectral Photographic Studies (S190).

After the first crew of three astronauts completes 28 days in Skylab, they will shut down all the systems on board the space station, crawl back through the airlock and tunnel into the Apollo Command Module, and return to Earth as in a normal Apollo flight re-entry. Some months later, the second crew will be launched into orbit, reach the workstation, complete their 56-day mission, and return. The eight-week mission of the third crew in 1973 is to bring Skylab I to a close and initiate the second phase of the Skylab Program: orbiting a second Skylab workstation and another succession of experiments.

All the while, each crew will be amassing a startling fund of information to be used for various purposes, including the planning, building and orbiting of a space station much larger than Skylab. The two Skylab stations will be only a first major testing ground of what has been learned from manned space flight up to now. Putting into practice all the methods, systems and tools of space research developed up to 1972 will be a learning experience in itself.

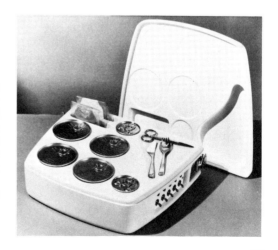

For the first time in space, Skylab astronauts will have frozen and conventional foods, along with dehydrated foods. The food tray will have separate compartments for canned foods, which will heat up quickly when a switch is thrown. Frozen foods, stored in freezers, will have to be preheated. Scissors are for cutting open the bags of dry and liquid foods.

LINEAR INDUCTION MOBILE HANDHOLD

PORTABLE HANDRAIL

Stations in Space

Men who plan for the future in space make use of what has been termed the "building principle" in which each subsequent step in planning relies upon what has gone before. By following such a step-by-step plan, each piece of equipment is first tested, then modified to become more functional, and finally used in actual flight. Essentially, this is what will happen to Skylab. It will become enlarged, necessary changes in its structure will be made, and it will be designed to hold more people.

To keep costs to a minimum, space scientists have adopted the cylinder as the basic form of the space station. The cylinder can be easily carried by rocket or even be part of the rocket itself. Since there is no atmosphere in space to provide lift and drag for aircraft wings, the actual shape of a space station is of no consequence aerodynamically. Commenting on this principle, a space engineer remarked, "Man's future in space depends upon how well he can adapt the cylinder for human use and habitation. The cylinder is the easiest to transport, the most economical and the most space-saving configuration. We're literally going to march across the universe on a series of tin cans."

Plans are for the large Space Station to consist of a basic cylinder capable of holding 6 to 12 men comfortably. It will be designed so that other large cylinders can be attached to it. Each cylinder is to be launched separately and brought into identical orbit with the other cylinder(s), and then all the cylinders are to be latched together. Eventually as many as 50 men are

INFLATABLE MID-TORSO RESTRAINT

LEG RAIL RESTRAINT

In Skylab's zero-G gravity, portable handrails and special restraint devices will enable the weightless astronauts to move about a large space station or remain in place.

expected to live and work at one space station complex made up of many cylinders all linked together. The Station will then be a floating city in space. The city will be known to spacemen as a Space Base, and may eventually be enlarged further to house as many as 100 men.

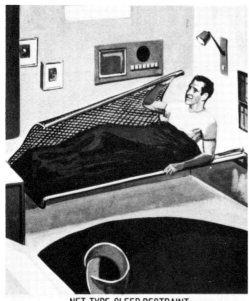

NET-TYPE SLEEP RESTRAINT

SUCTION SHOES

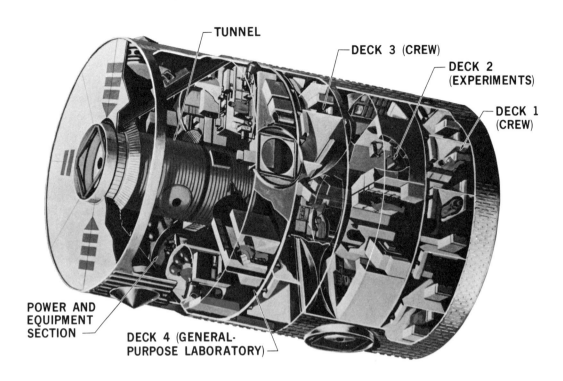

TUNNEL

DECK 3 (CREW)

DECK 2 (EXPERIMENTS)

DECK 1 (CREW)

POWER AND EQUIPMENT SECTION

DECK 4 (GENERAL-PURPOSE LABORATORY)

SPACE STATION CORE MODULE

DECKS 1 & 3: Crew quarters and operations: 6 crew quarter sections each deck with desk, chair, lamps, wardrobe, cot; 1 galley each deck with stove, refrigeration, waste removal, storage; 1 wardroom each deck for eating/conference/entertainment (movies); 1 shower; 2 waste management sections; 1 operations control center with television, tape decks, radio communication, on-board computers, monitoring equipment; 1 electrical distribution section; 1 airlock.

DECK 4: General Purpose Laboratory: experiment and test isolation facility for space physics, material processing and advanced technology; optics facility for astronomy, space physics, Earth observation, material processing; data processing facility for information gathering; mechanical laboratory for all purposes and processes; electronic laboratory for servicing, repair and research; 2 airlocks.

DECK 2: Experiment laboratories: biomedical, bioscience, dispensary, isolation facility, data evaluation laboratory, man-system integration laboratory, 1 airlock.

The Space Station is to be a combination hotel and research center, carrying on much the same kind of work that was done in Skylab but on a much larger and more advanced basis. Equally important for spacemen will be the ability to repair and re-use equipment right on board the station to save time and the expense of always having new equipment ferried back and forth from Earth. Scientists will be able to spend long periods of time at the station conducting lengthy experimentation and studying hundreds of different phenomena. The long life of the station will reduce its cost considerably. The station will pay for itself over a period of many years once it becomes fixed in space. Also, space engineers and technicans can repair the station if it should suffer damage from meteors or from spacecraft docking accidents.

The Space Station design concept, called a Baseline Space Station, depends upon a two-deck common module plan which is the basic building block of the entire space station program. Two of these modules fitted together make an ideal large-area station. Other two-deck modules could either orbit separately or be permanently attached to the station.

The common module is planned to be 33 feet in diameter and is to be divided into two decks. The module will contain a full life-support system. Two modules, comprising four decks, will contain the work and living areas; two decks will be devoted to laboratory space and the other two decks used for operations and living quarters. Provisions have been made for data processing and evaluation, testing and calibrating of optical systems, sleeping and dressing quarters, exercising area, waste removal, kitchen, biomedical experiments section, photographic facilities, etc. The station will periodically receive other unmanned free-flying scientific modules for servicing and maintenance.

The modular station is designed for zero gravity, or weightlessness, but it also has a capability for switching to artificial gravity. Crews will be rotated back to Earth every 90 days to be tested for the physiological results of artificial gravity. The station will have a circular Earth orbit of about 242 nautical miles. A central pressurized tunnel running the length of the station will serve as the main traffic artery so crew members can move from deck to deck, entering each deck through a 5-foot diameter opening. The tunnel also will serve as an emergency refuge area in case one of the station compartments has to be evacuated. Each module will accommodate 12 men (in two decks) so that the station of four decks will have ample room for moving about without feeling cramped. Seldom will more than 12 men permanently inhabit the station.

Outside the craft, a meteoroid bumper will ward off bombardment from large and small meteors. The hull of the station will serve as a radiator shell which will prevent radiation penetration. The shell is designed to repel meteoroid puncture for at least 10 years with a 99 per cent probability of success.

The station has seven docking ports, five on the cylindrical surface and one at each end. Each port has a 5-foot access door and an atmosphere seal as well as hinged covers to provide thermal and meteoroid protection.

The Main Space Station crew, consisting of a Station Commander and three other astronaut/engineers, is responsible for maintaining and operating the station. The remainder of the 12-man contingent will be under the

Food for astronauts in orbit must be contained in enclosed packages to prevent their drifting about during weightless periods in space.

direction of a Chief Scientist who is the ultimate authority for all experimentation. There will not be a physician on board. All crew members, while having a 12-hour "responsibility" in shifts, will work a normal 8-hour day. This type of duty procedure has worked successfully in the U.S. armed forces for decades.

The station is designed to operate entirely on its own for 180 days, with 90-day crew rotations. Each new crew will bring aboard supplies for 180 days. Artificial gravity will be attained by "swinging" the station, counterbalancing it with the spent Saturn S-II stage attached to the station by long cables. The free-flying experiment modules will not be manned but will be capable of automatic self-propulsion under the direction of the station crew.

Putting the Baseline Space Station into full operation will require 12 initial flights. The first launch will put the empty station in orbit. Then, by a specially designed Shuttle Craft, the 12-man crew will be flown up to the station. Additional shuttle flights then will ferry supplies and provisions to the station and return with equipment that cannot be re-used, as well as tape-stored data. Over the 10-year lifetime of the station, about 41 such Shuttle flights will be required to maintain the station.

The Baseline Space Station concept is vitally important for the future success of man in space because it is the concept round which all stations will be built, including stations that are expected to be placed in orbit ultimately round other planets. The first station will be a test station to determine if the concept is sufficient and safe. No one knows what new developments will occur within the station itself. Scientists are excited about the many possibilities and the future potential of the experiments to be carried out aboard the space station. The space station described here is to become an important link between the Earth and the Moon—a sort of "half-way" station for men and supplies coming and going between lunar bases and colonies.

This Mobile Geological Laboratory, which weighs 8 tons, is built for rugged terrain. Created to test instruments under simulated conditions, for astronauts going to the Moon, it can also perform support missions and may become a basic design for future lunar and Mars trucks.

The Space Shuttle

The success and versatility of the Space Station depends upon continual re-supply and crew rotation. To accomplish these tasks, a re-usable craft had to be designed that was economical to launch and capable of being put into service over and over again. The concept of a Space Shuttle Craft emerged from the thinking of aeronautical engineers and NASA planners as an answer to the problems of staggeringly high costs and spacecraft endurance, as well as the obvious tasks involved in ferrying men and supplies into space.

The Space Shuttle will attach to a manned rocket plane that will carry the Space Shuttle to a high altitude. The rocket plane and its "piggy-back" Shuttle will take off vertically from a pad similar to the one at Cape Kennedy, and will be aimed for Earth-orbit. When the plane's fuel is nearly exhausted (in about 3 minutes), it will let loose the Shuttle Craft which will then operate on its own power—with no sonic boom—to attain orbital velocity while the rocket plane returns to Earth and makes a horizontal landing at the site from which it was launched, like any normal winged aircraft. This "slingshot effect" can be used with the same rocket plane carrying Shuttle Craft in as many successive boosts as necessary. Both the plane and the Shuttle Craft are re-usable, a highly important factor in cost reduction.

The Shuttle will carry up to 50,000 pounds of payload, including passengers and cargo intermixed, on both flights of a round-trip mission to the Space

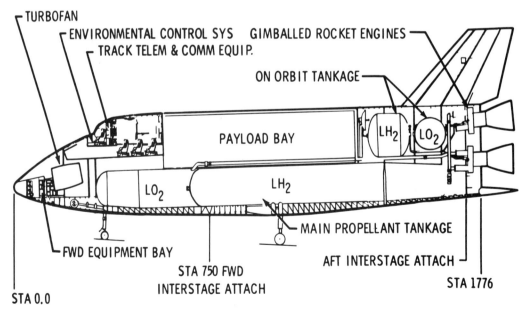

Cutaway sketch of the Shuttle Orbiter. Note the size of the crew and passengers compared to the over-all size of the craft.

In this artist's rendering of the Space Shuttle, the "Orbiter" portion is on top, heading for its objective in space just after it has separated from the "Booster," which will now glide down to an Earth landing.

Station. The cargo compartment will be about 15 feet in diameter and about 60 feet long. The Shuttle itself is capable of re-entry and conventional landing on a horizontal runway like an ordinary aircraft. Normal flights are expected to require a week; stay at the Space Station another 10 days to two weeks; and the return trip a week. The craft is designed for a lifetime of at least 100 flights or longer. Burning liquid hydrogen and liquid oxygen, its engines can develop a thrust of 400,000 pounds each to carry the Shuttle's weight of close to 3,500,000 pounds at launch.

The Shuttle Craft is the kingpin in the Space Station concept, whether the station is in Earth orbit, lunar orbit or the orbit of another planet. Acting as an air transport vehicle, it will be outfitted, repaired and maintained like most conventional airplanes. Landing will be completely automated. The vehicle will require only a normal ground servicing crew, will be operated by a pilot and co-pilot, and will be monitored by both spacecraft guidance systems and a small ground control staff. After the initial experience with the take-off and landing operations, these activities will later be designed to take place at conventional airports.

The Shuttle Craft will be modified later to facilitate landing and take-off from the Moon, or from other planets. Designed to dock with the Space Station, it will dock with a station anywhere in the Solar System, making

PASSENGER AND CREW TRANSPORTATION

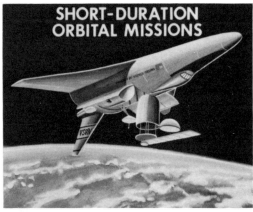

SHORT-DURATION ORBITAL MISSIONS

RESCUE

PROPULSION STAGES DELIVERY

The various types of missions to be carried out by the Shuttle Orbiter.

possible long flights to other planets. Carrying 12 passengers, who can relax in a shirt-sleeve environment much like that of commercial airliners of today, the Shuttle will permit ferrying of men who need no astronaut training and won't ever have to wear a space suit. Shuttles will eventually travel back and forth on a schedule like today's airlines.

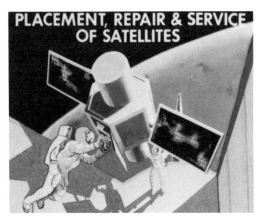

PLACEMENT, REPAIR & SERVICE OF SATELLITES

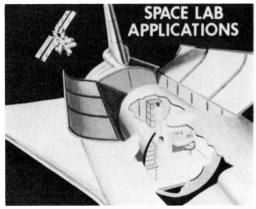

SPACE LAB APPLICATIONS

While the general public will not be permitted seats on Shuttle Craft, the use of the vehicle will entirely revolutionize our present concepts of space travel. Occupational specialists—photographers, writers, engineers, technicians and research scientists—will find space travel more desirable and considerably more pleasant than ever believed possible. The Shuttle may very well make space travel as convenient as a normal business trip, and as the number of Space Stations increases, so will the demand grow for Shuttle Craft.

The Craft will have to pass through developmental speed stages of subsonic, sonic, supersonic and finally hypersonic—many times faster than the speed of sound. At such speeds, the Craft will have to endure great stress and its engines will have to be capable of immediate starting and stopping. With this kind of design, the Shuttle will be launched on a few hours notice, as in the case of space emergencies. It will be used for very quick transportation flights between two points on the Earth's surface, or the surface of another planet. This will allow ferrying passengers from New York to Tokyo or Australia in an hour or less.

This artist's painting shows two robots preparing to inspect a Shuttle Craft in space before its re-entry into the Earth's atmosphere. The television-camera-laden robots are controlled by astronauts inside another Shuttle Orbiter.

In this painting, the artist shows a remote-controlled robot inspecting and preparing a Nimbus satellite which has just been launched into orbit from the Shuttle Orbiter, from which the robot is also controlled.

Plans are for the Space Shuttle to deliver a module for a permanent space station. The re-usable Shuttle will deliver many of these modules in a week's time and completely build a space station in orbit piece by piece.

A Space Station completely built from separate modules delivered to orbit by the Shuttle Craft.

Large Space Bases

The Baseline Space Station described in this section is composed of two separate common modules, each module having two decks. If perhaps as many as 20 modules were attached together in a long line, it would furnish 40 decks and working and living quarters for over 200 people. This concept is possible in the 21st century, but for the remainder of the 20th century a large Space Base housing 50 to 100 people is quite within the realm of possibility and is being planned now. The Space Shuttle Craft will make it possible.

The large Space Base is an outgrowth of the "expansion sequence" of building big stations in space, which works like this: Once a typical Space Station is in orbit (having four decks), a second Station is then launched and the two Stations become linked together providing a 24-man complex. As other modules are attached, nuclear reactor power plants can be permanently hitched to the complex. Next, by adding a central hub, other Space Station units and nuclear plants can be added until the entire configuration becomes

33

Shuttle Orbiter on its rocket Booster plane prepared for launch.

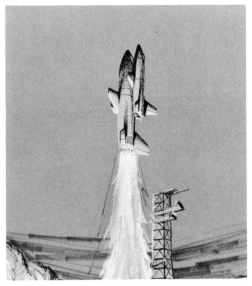

Piggy-back launch of the rocket Booster and the Shuttle Orbiter.

Here is how Shuttle Orbiter passengers sit during launch.

Staging (separation) of Booster and Orbiter.

Orbiter beginning rendezvous with Space Station already in orbit.

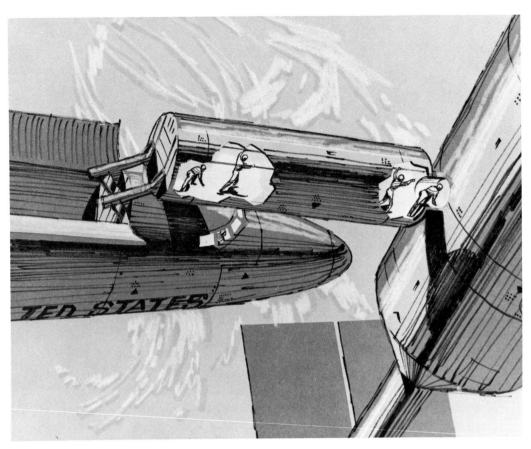

After docking at Space Station the crew transfers through the airlock.

a large, expanded base operated by 100 or so scientists. The Space Base can either be rotated for artificial gravity or remain a nonrotating, "Zero-G" Base; even a combination of both types of gravity is possible.

Nuclear reactors and solar cell panels are vital for the large base. The power supply to keep the base operational must be constant and never-ending. For this reason, the nuclear power plant seems to be the best possible source. Cost again is important. Nuclear power, once adapted for conventional use, will be far more economical and reliable than gathering solar energy by means of solar array panels.

When fully developed, the expanded Space Base can be constructed anywhere in the universe! The implications for such a capability are astounding, and open up so many possibilities that in the 1970's we have a difficult time comprehending exactly what it all means. A Space Base in Saturn orbit, for example, would allow unlimited opportunity to study that planet for extended periods. Capable of changing its orbital altitude and inclination plane, such a Space Base would have virtually no limitations for scientific investigation.

Orbiter craft returns to horizontal landing on Earth like a conventional airplane.

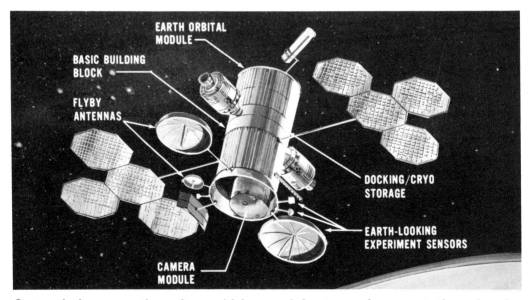

One artist's conception of an orbiting modular type of space station, showing solar cell panels and docked Apollo Command and Service Modules.

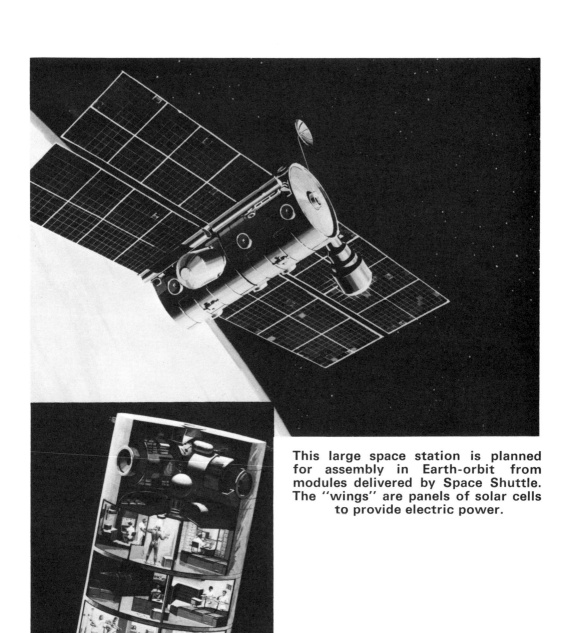

This large space station is planned for assembly in Earth-orbit from modules delivered by Space Shuttle. The "wings" are panels of solar cells to provide electric power.

Cutaway view of a proposed 12-man Space Station with three decks.

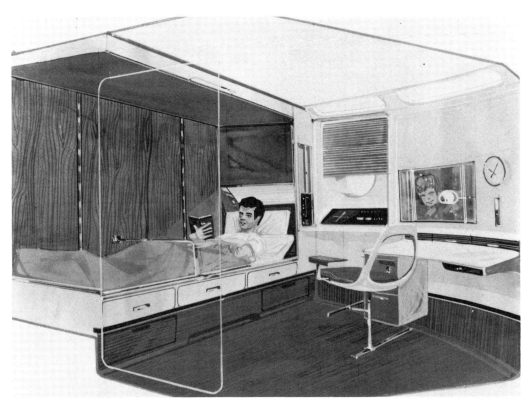

In the shirt-sleeve environment of the Space Station, living and sleeping quarters will be cheerful, in an atmosphere of quiet and privacy.

Artificial gravity can be supplied to a Space Station when the entire complex rotates on its axis, as in this artist's sketch of a future Space Base containing up to 300 scientists, astronauts and professional services personnel.

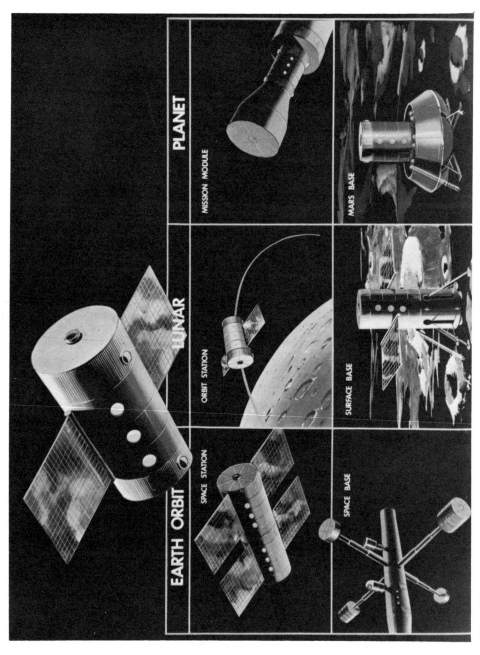

Modules can be joined to form (1) Space Stations, (2) Moon orbit stations, (3) missions to Mars and other planets, (4) space bases, (5) floors of a Moon surface base, and (6) a base on Mars.

Another use for the modules is as an orbiting astronomy/telescope that is compatible with the Space Station and the Shuttle.

Lunar Surface Bases

If men are going to use the Moon to advantage, they will have to learn how to live on it. The first lunar bases, like the first orbiting space stations, will be test concepts utilizing the knowledge gained from the Apollo landing flights and from the first space stations. The first lunar base will be a shelter— a large, stationary, upright structure capable of housing a crew of six scientists who will be able to leave the shelter at will. This "shelter" concept will be expanded to include a number of similar lunar surface structures clustered in many different places.

The first step toward establishing a lunar base will be the Apollo follow-up program with the goal of establishing several lunar orbit space stations whose crews can move freely back and forth between lunar orbit and lunar surface during a period of several weeks. Lunar exploration crews will make repeated three-day trips down to the Moon's surface to investigate the terrain and

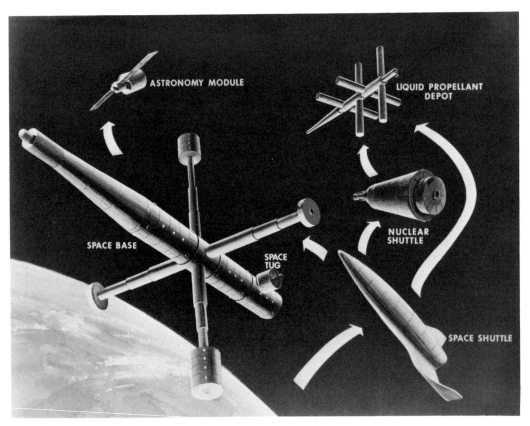

Large Space Bases for 100 men or more can be constructed by linking many Station Modules together.

other lunar features. After several weeks have passed, the lunar orbit station crew will return to Earth and a new crew will be sent to the station.

The concept of lunar orbit station and rotating crews could be accomplished by the mid- to late-1970's according to present plans. The lunar orbit station is to be essentially the same kind of station as the Earth orbit station, except that the lunar surface shelter will house the crew while it is investigating the Moon.

By 1980, using the typical space cylinder, a Lunar Surface Base for six men at first is expected to be sent to the Moon's surface. This will permit longer staytime, wider ranges of exploration, automated Rover vehicle traverses, increased supply and equipment transport, and also allow explorers to bring back much larger loads of lunar material for analysis. The permanent Lunar Base Station will be essentially the same configuration as the Baseline Space Station except the station itself will need to have landing/stabilizing legs as part of its design.

To meet the requirements of the Lunar Surface Base, much existing equipment will have to be considerably improved. Space suits will have to allow freer human movement; life-support back packs must contain larger supplies of oxygen; all equipment must be more compact and of much lighter weight. The Rover vehicle so successfully tested first on the Apollo 15 flight in 1971 will be modified to fulfil a dual rôle—as a man-carrying vehicle able to travel over wide areas, and as an automatic vehicle controlled by a console located inside the Base.

New information discovered by Rover will have to be relayed directly from the vehicle to Earth, Earth-orbit Space Station, and the Lunar Surface Base simultaneously. While the Lunar Base is unattended (for example, during crew rotation periods), the Rover must be capable of being controlled directly from Earth or from an orbiting Space Station.

Clusters of Lunar Surface Base stations will assume the appearance of small "villages" on the Moon powered by nuclear-energy power plants. The scientists in these villages will conduct highly technical research in a potentially threatening environment where disaster can strike any moment. Huddled

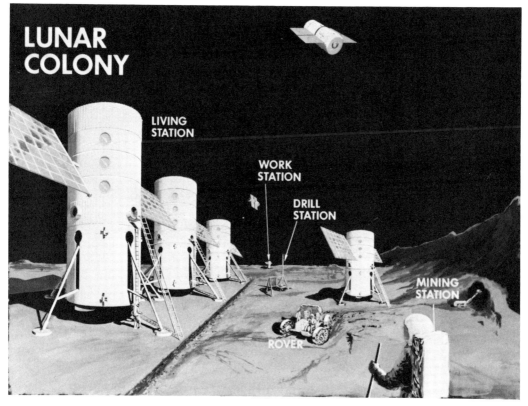

This concept of a Lunar Colony actually has an assembly of Space Station modules modified to become permanent structures. However, they have to be capable of lifting off from the Moon in the event of emergencies. This scene may be a reality well before the year 2000. If begun now, it could be finished in the early 1980's.

together on the alien surface of such a body in space, these men will have needs highly unlike those of people anywhere else. For protection, ease of mobility, scientific investigation, personal hygiene, psychological safety and immediate communication, many new systems will have to be devised. Each new set of design problems must be solved in turn before men can move farther out into space, and become creatures of the universe.

The whole surface of the Moon must be available for exploration. This means that the entire surface must eventually be made habitable for man, with hundreds of Moon Bases dotting the lunarscape. Each shelter will be really nothing more than a small house equivalent to the modular Baseline Space Station; here several men can live and work, and leave occasionally for forages across the lunar terrain. While the shelter type of base is sufficient for initial explorations involving days or weeks, a much more sophisticated base is needed for permanent colonization and for sustained exploration and research. Only then can man make the Moon truly his home-away-from-home.

Exploring the Moon

The same work that geologists and rockhounds do on Earth must be performed on the Moon. The greatest difference lies in the fact that Earth-bound man can perform this work naturally in a known environment. On the Moon, though, he will be continually hampered and restricted all along the way because of the Moon's alien environment. Instead of breathing freely, he will have to carry his own oxygen supply. He will have to be especially careful not to fall down, injure himself or rip open his life-giving space suit. He will have to carry his own heater and his own air conditioner—his own water supply and foodstuffs which he must be able to consume inside his space suit.

In the beginning there will be no road maps, and he will have to survey his prospecting area and chart it carefully before he can exploit it safely. He will have to become accustomed to great physical differences in this strange, new land. Distances are deceptively greater, rocks and crater beds sharp and steep, and walking in the ungainly loping manner characteristic of Moonwalkers will often be burdensome and tiring. The lunar "day" is 14 Earth days in length; so is the lunar "night." There are no clouds, no wind, no rain, no snow or frost, just Sun or no Sun. He will always see the same kind of landscape—rockpiles, craters, hills, valleys, depressions, mounds, cliffs, mountains. They will all be starkly obvious, for he will be able to see very clearly for great distances without the obscuring atmosphere of the Earth. Man will have to do a great deal of adjusting to his home on the Moon before he can explore it with confidence. There are no green meadows and sparkling streams to soothe his anxieties.

(Above) The Rover of Apollo 15 that cruised on the Moon, as it stood at the west edge of Mount Hadley. The Rover vehicle is an excellent example of how space engineers have solved the special problems of lunar travel. (Right) One of the wheels of the Rover, showing chevron-shaped treads of titanium riveted to the wire mesh around each wheel's outer circumference.

Astro-scientists have thousands of questions that must be answered about the Moon. They want to know everything there is to know, so the lunar explorers will be busy indeed. They will have to gather more and different kinds of rocks and lunar soil, charting their exact position before they are picked up. Man will literally investigate the Moon "inch by inch" because there are no lunar geology books. Scientists have already found that the moon dust brought back from the Apollo flights is more fertile than the Earth's earth, and also less attractive to insects.

Scientists hope to find some usable minerals on the Moon—perhaps deposits which can be mined or refined to make exploration financially worthwhile. Scientists will learn more about the Earth by learning more about the Moon. Inside each shelter laboratory, astronauts will have to test, analyze and become familiar with every bit of rock and soil near each base, because the site being explored is far different than the sites other explorers are studying 500 or 1,000 miles away.

Moon explorers will have to be excellent photographers and writers to record what they see and find, and make it all understood by those on Earth who have never walked on the Moon. Photography will be an invaluable aid in studying the Moon, especially color photography and stereoscopic views. Scientists will learn how the Moon was born, what it is made of, how old it is in different places, how old different formations are, what minerals are available there for man's present use, and what new future products can be made from lunar soil and its ingredients. Some scientists believe that the bacteria-free environment of the Moon will allow many products to be produced there faster, cheaper and more reliably.

The Shuttle Craft will be highly useful in exploring the Moon, as will Rover-type vehicles. Transportation, re-supply and cargo hauling in space, as well as on the lunar surface, are all necessary for exploration. Shuttle service between the Baseline Space Station and the lunar surface, between Earth and the Space Station, between two or more points on the Moon's surface, between the Lunar Surface Base and a lunar orbit Station, are all predicated on the development of successful Shuttle Craft service. It is not too soon to begin designing Lunar Buses and Trucks, along with single-man propulsion Manoeuvring Units to convey a single individual in space.

New Tools in Space

Many of the common, ordinary tools used in everyday life will function normally in space. Most will not. Confronted with the problems of weightlessness, small living quarters, oddly-shaped tools and devices, and the need for lightweight instruments, space explorers will need new tools designed for new tasks, as well as old tools redesigned for new and old tasks. Each tool will have to be separately tested and perfected before it can be used as standard equipment.

When you are in a swimming pool and try to push or pull an object that floats, you find it difficult. The reason is that the buoyancy of the water greatly reduces not only the weight, but the stability of both the object and your own body. The same thing happens in the weightless environment of space where a floating space engineer finds he must tighten or loosen bolts, hammer a piece of gear, or turn screws—and can't because he has no stable surface to stand upon or push against. A basic law of physics is that for every action there is an equal and opposite reaction. How true this is in space!

A *plench* is a combination pliers and wrench which allows the user to turn a nut while floating freely. The pliers portion of the tool grips the nut tightly so the user won't be pushed away when he tries to turn. The wrench portion is motor driven, allowing the user to remain in a stationary position. Similarly, a *spammer* is a space hammer which attaches to the surface of the object to be pounded. An automatic hammering head inside the spammer does its own work so the user doesn't have to swing his arm back and forth. Adapting present tools for use in space, however, is the easiest part of solving the problem.

The Apollo astronauts had to learn how to use many new kinds of tools on their Moon expeditions—old tools designed for old tasks which had to be performed in a new way. Core drills for obtaining samples from deep inside

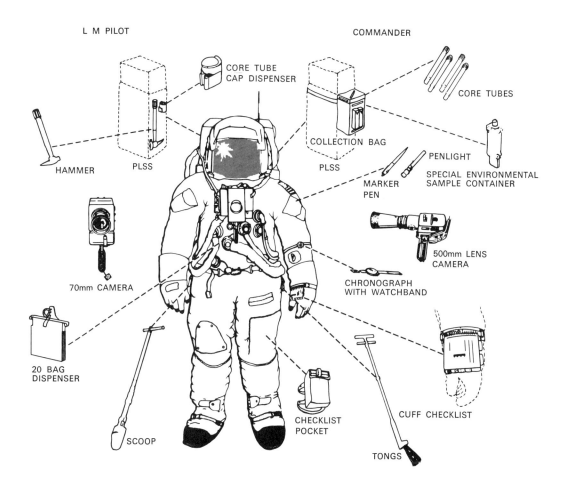

LM PILOT   COMMANDER

CORE TUBE CAP DISPENSER

CORE TUBES

COLLECTION BAG

PENLIGHT

MARKER PEN

SPECIAL ENVIRONMENTAL SAMPLE CONTAINER

HAMMER   PLSS   PLSS

500mm LENS CAMERA

70mm CAMERA

CHRONOGRAPH WITH WATCHBAND

20 BAG DISPENSER

CUFF CHECKLIST

CHECKLIST POCKET

SCOOP

TONGS

The tools, instruments and devices used by Apollo 15 astronauts (shown here) will serve for many years to come, but eventually will be modified and changed, as experience is gained.

the lunar surface had to be sharper and designed so that when the drill turned it wouldn't also turn the astronaut holding onto it. Man on the Moon weighs only one sixth what he weighs on Earth. The problem was solved by a special drill that revolved much more slowly.

The light weight of an instrument is a problem, as discovered by Apollo astronauts who found it all too easy to knock down various pieces of equipment they had taken a long time to set up. Even the flagpole for the American flag had to be specially designed because, without an atmosphere on the Moon to provide a breeze for unfurling the flag, the fabric simply hung straight down and couldn't be seen. A folding arm that jutted out from the flagpole at a 90°-angle was devised to keep the flag stretched out.

Moon rocks have much sharper surfaces than do rocks on Earth because wind, rain, snow and flying debris do not beat against them and smooth them over. There is a lunar ground-covering of fine, sandlike soil which in some

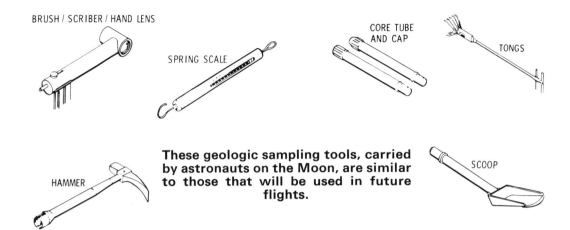

BRUSH / SCRIBER / HAND LENS

SPRING SCALE

CORE TUBE AND CAP

TONGS

HAMMER

These geologic sampling tools, carried by astronauts on the Moon, are similar to those that will be used in future flights.

SCOOP

places has been found a foot or more deep. The Rover vehicle's tires had to be designed to withstand difficulties of rolling across these areas. With no rain or hard winds, it isn't really necessary for a Moon car to have a roof or sides although a roof and sides would protect the riders from micro-meteoroid particles and the harsh glare of the Sun. Future trucks and cars will have to contend with very steep sides of craters, uneven and rocky lunar terrain, "sandy" stretches of lunarscape, and the fact that internal combustion engines can't be used on the Moon since there is no oxygen there.

To overcome such obstacles, engineers have designed double-thick tank trucks to withstand meteor bombardment and blazing heat; thick coverings for telescopes, solar batteries and other instruments; and special boots and wearing apparel for the astronauts. Communication units, water and oxygen supply containers, storage sheds and even flashlights must be re-designed to a certain extent.

Space engineers will also be called upon to design new tools for events and objects which man has not yet encountered. Astronauts may find, for example, that a spacecraft travelling through space needs an unconventional windshield wiper to wipe away clinging gases, space dust, burnt meteoroid particles, or even strange liquids and growths found on other planets. On-board systems will also have to be re-designed and put to new uses. Probably the most important aspect in re-design is to make an object as simple as possible, right from the start, so that repairs can be made quickly and with a minimum of small parts. Storage space aboard space stations, bases, craft and unmanned vehicles is extremely precious. Engineers now believe that having a repair "replacement module" is no longer an efficient plan, because the replacement module itself takes up too much space.

The fields of medicine, electronics, photography and administrative management have benefitted most from the space program. Devices and systems created for the space program have found their way into general

SPACE SHUTTLE: This is the Orbiter after it has been launched by riding piggy-back for three minutes on a rocket Booster, which has returned to Earth like a plane. The Shuttle, too, will eventually return as a plane, landing on a runway of 10,000 feet or more. Saving the two parts of the Space Shuttle reduces costs significantly. The Orbiter, in this artist's conception, with a crew of four, has deployed a Nimbus weather satellite. A tethered space technician has crawled out of the open bay to perform check-out tasks. The Orbiter weighs some 900,000 lbs. and is expected to be in operation during the mid-1970's, as Congress has appropriated funds for its construction.

A

SKYLAB: This Manned Orbital Scientific Space Station (its official name), to be launched in the mid-1970's, is going to make use of the knowledge gained by the Mercury–Gemini–Apollo missions to try to obtain further scientific, medical and technological information in three areas: locating the Earth's resources from space, medical data on man's living in space, and astronomical facts about the Sun, especially. Solar batteries power the Skylab in space. Note them and the large telescope peeking out. If the Skylab project is successful, it will lead to maintaining permanent Space Stations.

B

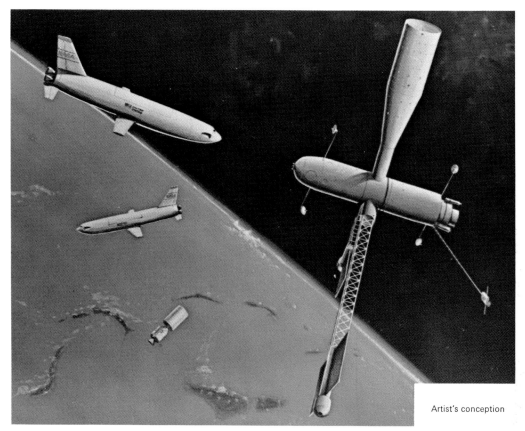

Artist's conception

SHUTTLE APPROACHES SPACE STATION: In Earth orbit, the Station inhabitants have just seen one Shuttle depart for Earth as another (top left) approaches. Below is an earlier generation space workshop. The re-usable Shuttle is expected to transport men, supplies and equipment between Earth and all Space Stations of the future.

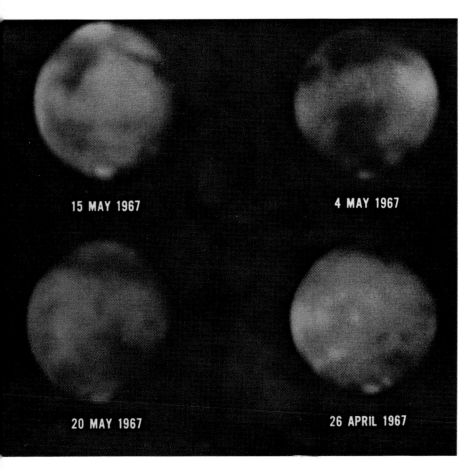

15 MAY 1967

4 MAY 1967

20 MAY 1967

26 APRIL 1967

MARS:
The **NASA**
telescope
took these
color views.

**MARS
EXCURSION
MODULE: It**
has landed on
desert-like
terrain, where
its two
astronauts
have set up a
portable
meteorolog-
ical station
and a 10-foot
antenna for
communica-
tion.

Concept developed by
Aeronutronic Division
of the Philco-Ford
Corp., Newport Beach,
Calif.

D

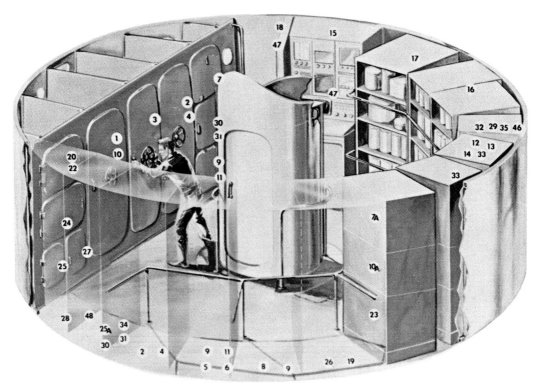

EARTH RESOURCES LABORATORY: With the following equipment, this orbiting station can perform a multitude of tasks:

1	Metric Cameras	20	Infra-Red Scanning Spectrometer
2	High Resolution Panoramic Cameras	21	Interferometers
		22	Ultra-Violet Photometer
3	Multi-Spectral Tracking Telescope	23	Microwave Radiometer
		24	Infra-Red Radiometer-Multichannel
4	Synoptic Multi-Band Cameras	25	TV Camera
5	High Resolution Radar Imager	26	Radar System (Infra-Red)
6	Radar Altimeter/Scatterometer	27	High Resolution Infra-Red Camera (6″ Aperture)
7	Wide Range Spectral Scanner		
8	Passive Microwave Imaging	28	SFERICS Receiver
9	Ultra-Violet Spectrometer	29	Additional Equipment Storage Bay
10	Laser/Altimeter Scatterometer		
11	Absorption Spectroscopy	30	Infra-Red Scanner/Radiometer
12	Radio Frequency Reflectivity	31	Visible Spectrometer
13	Magnetometer	32	High Resolution Star Tracking
14	Gravity Gradiometer	33	Auxiliary Equipment Storage Bay
15	Earth Resources Support Equipment	34	Microwave Scanning Radiometer
		35	Ultra-Violet Photometer
16	Film Storage Cannisters	46	Low Energy Cosmic Rays
17	Spare Parts	47	Magnetic Tape Units (16 Req'd)
18	Magnetic Tape Units (6 Req'd)	48	Electronic Support Equipment
19	Film Processing Equipment		

F

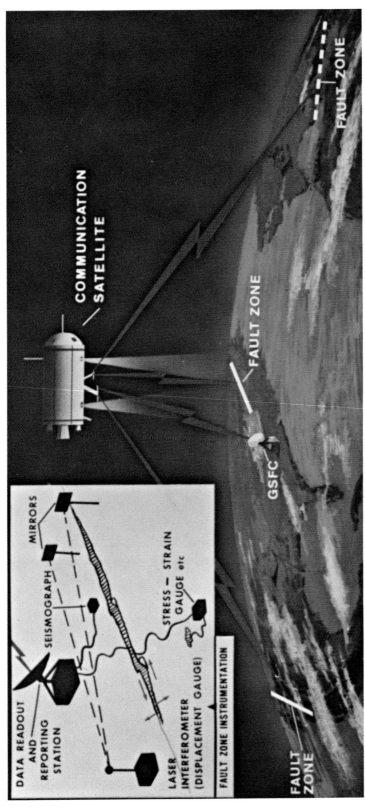

EARTHQUAKE PREDICTOR: This Orbiting Communications Satellite can locate areas in the Earth's crust where cracks or faults lie near or below the surface. Other orbiting satellites and stations searching for resources on Earth have sensors attuned to finding oil, gas, metals, thermal forces, underground rivers, and even where vegetables grow best or have plant diseases.

MODULAR SPACE STATION: Cutaway view shows the living quarters and laboratories of an Earth-orbiting semi-permanent station that can be launched in parts and assembled in space. It is planned to have a life of 10 years. The modules are rotational to simulate gravitation and allow a shirt-sleeve environment inside.

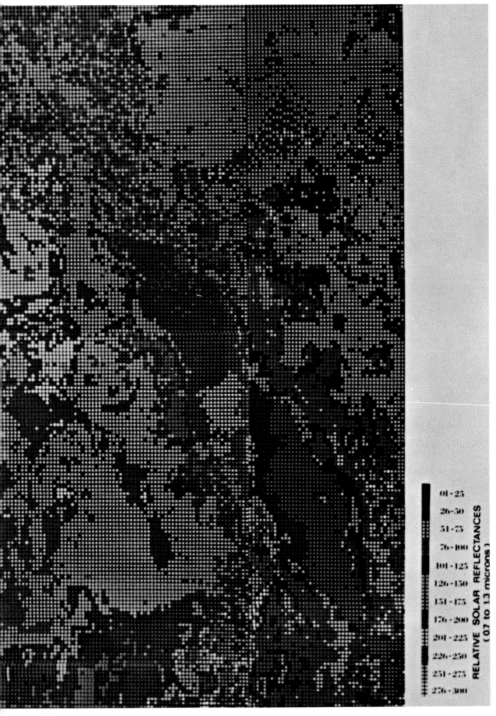

RELATIVE SOLAR REFLECTANCES
(07 to 1.3 microns)

	01 - 25
	26 - 50
	51 - 75
	76 - 100
	101 - 125
	126 - 150
	151 - 175
	176 - 200
	201 - 225
	226 - 250
	251 - 275
	276 - 300

INFRARED MAP from space: This reflectance picture was taken by the Nimbus III high resolution infra-red radiometer (HRIR) and shows the area around the Red Sea (blue), with Saudi Arabia on the right and northeast Africa on the left. The colors indicate the amount of vegetation, metal, oil, etc. as seen in the Sun's reflectance.

H

industry where they are beginning to revolutionize the tools used by man on Earth. If one often wonders why the United States can send two men to the Moon yet not solve some major problems here on Earth, the answer is that many everyday problems *are* being solved. The benefits from the space effort are staggering—but we know little about them because many are highly technical. Some of them include:

A special coating intended for satellites, but with many other uses, that can withstand temperatures as high as 1,300° F (704° C) or as low as 320° F (160° C) below zero.

A 24-ounce, battery-operated TV camera the size of a king-size pack of cigarettes, invented to photograph separation of the Saturn rocket stages that is useful in many tight situations.

Self-lubricating materials made for space purposes that now allow industry to produce ball bearings and other moving parts that last far longer.

A tiny instrument to measure air pressure on rocket models in wind tunnels that can be injected into the bloodstream of a patient with a hypodermic needle to send out information about a patient's heart.

A tiny TV camera that can be safely swallowed to show whether a patient has ulcers or stomach ailments.

A special meter that measures astronauts' bone conditions after periods of weightlessness and is being applied to the study of brittle bones in elderly patients.

An electronic switch that can be controlled simply by movement of the eyes, when attached to a pair of goggles or eyeglasses. Prepared for astronauts in case they cannot move their heads or hands, the switch, controlled by tiny light beams that measure the difference between the pupil and white part of the eye, is triggered when the eyes are moved.

Devices designed to help astronauts walk on the Moon with little gravity that can help crippled people walk again.

An invention that measures micro-meteoroid strikes and is so sensitive it can detect the slightest muscular tremor, that will be used to discover early signs of certain muscular diseases.

The use of moon dust by botanists to help grow corn that is, as a result, impervious to pests.

Significant advances have been made in communications, weather monitoring and prediction, and in Earth resources detection and repair. In addition, industry is highly interested in an orbiting factory which can grow perfect, giant crystals that would supplant thousands of tiny electronic components used in computers, transistor radios and television sets. Scientists calculate one such spaceflight per month would supply the world's requirements for crystals.

A Day at Mare Imbrium

In the early 1950's, the science fiction writers predicted that Mare Imbrium in the Moon's upper left quadrant would be of prime interest to science because of the many possibilities surrounding its unusual formation and development and its suitability as a smooth landing site. Although Project Apollo planners did not choose Mare Imbrium for one of the Apollo missions, those early fiction writers were still not far from wrong. Scientists are very much interested in the area and may well decide to establish a base there. We can now only imagine what it will be like to work on the Moon for several weeks at a time, but very soon, by 1980, it may become a reality. Let's suppose a team of scientists is ready to land there. Before they can go . . .

Two manned Apollo-type missions will already have been to Mare Imbrium in the 1970's. Space Station L-4 in lunar orbit will have carefully photographed the area with three different types of films, including infrared. The pictures will have to be much better than any ever taken of the Moon. The two Apollo teams, passing information and film cartridges back and forth to the Station scientists, will have assembled several volumes of material which the Imbrium-bound team will have studied for six months. Now, with a fully loaded cargo compartment, the crew will be ferried by Shuttle from Baseline Station SS-7 to the orbiting Lunar Station L-4 passing 65 miles above the landing site.

After the Shuttle docks at L-4 and the three-man Imbrium crew transfers to the Lunar Station, final checks will be made of equipment, provisions, cargo, life-support and communications systems. The Shuttle will wait at dock until a Lunar Base Shelter has been automatically landed at Mare Imbrium by computer. The Shelter will be on its way by rocket. It will arrive during Earth night and will be guided automatically by L-4 personnel into its proper position on the lunar surface below.

The next morning, the crew will be ferried to the Moon's surface by Crew Module which is programmed to return to L-4, receive the cargo from the Shuttle, and then return to the fledgling Base. During the morning period, the crew will assemble equipment and check it, putting the Lunar Surface Shelter into operational status. Communications will be established with several main points; Lunar Station L-4, Baseline Space Station SS-9, Cape Kennedy, Houston Manned Space Flight Center, and another Lunar Surface Base at the crater Archimedes.

Through the viewing port, the Shelter Commander will be able to see LaPlace Promontory looming on the horizon about 15 miles away. Tomorrow, he expects a second Lunar Shelter to arrive with a Ground Bus and a pair of Crew Manoeuvring Units for individual travel. He will guide the landing of the second Shelter to relieve the personnel in L-4 to do other tasks.

The crew of three will leave the safety of their own Base Shelter for the

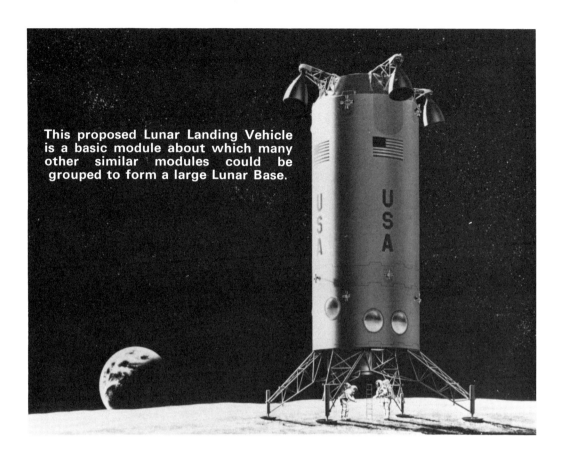

This proposed Lunar Landing Vehicle is a basic module about which many other similar modules could be grouped to form a large Lunar Base.

first time to connect power and monitoring cables from equipment put in place many weeks before by the last Apollo explorer team. Seismometer, radiometer, solar energy-gathering cell cluster, communications antennae, ground-earth television, micro-meteoroid counter, temperature gauges and nuclear power plant will all be put in readiness. The Lunar Shelter, primitive start of what will become a huge Lunar Surface Base, will now be in full operation.

The Base Commander will be an Astronaut/Engineer who will later direct the building and expansion of the Base. The crew will also include an Astronaut/Geologist who will serve as the Base Executive Officer and second in command. The third crew member, a Geophysicist, will be the Base Chief Science Officer once the other crews and equipment arrive. These three men will remain at the Base for three months before they are rotated to Lunar Station L-4 for a one-month tour and then home to Earth.

The secondary mission of this first crew will be to direct all the activities and research of the Base's eventual 42 scientists in a concentrated study of the terrain, rock formations and composition, including seismic experiments and geographical distribution of the areas known as LaPlace Promontory, the Straight Range, and the Jura Mountains. Samples will be ferried by

Astronaut Alan B. Shepard trains for his Apollo 14 mission with a stereo camera while wearing an Extra-vehicular Mobility Unit. The unit will be modified as experience dictates, to make the gear smaller and lighter.

Crew Module up to Station L-4 where they will be taken by Shuttle to Station SS-9 for test and analysis. Color, black-and-white and stereoscopic photo views will be sent to the Center For Lunar and Planetary Studies at the University of Arizona for map making and other research.

A four-minute warning light and buzzer will indicate suddenly to the crew that the first six-hour recording tape will run out in approximately four minutes. It will have to be replaced with a fresh tape. The crew members will begin to go about their various tasks of planning for the expansion of the Imbrium Base. They have been told to expect a Lunar Ferry at 1700 hours from the nearest Lunar Base at Archimedes with a prize—a 90-minute entertainment film for the enjoyment of the crew. Imbrium Base will keep the film for two weeks before returning it. In the meantime, other films will be sent to the Imbrium Base from Station SS-9, the Imbrium Base's main service and supply point.

The crew will feel a bit more at ease to know that there is a medical staff at Archimedes Base, as well as emergency equipment and immediate re-supply of life-support materials, should an urgency arise. Since Archimedes is only six minutes away by Ferry, one of the crew will visit the base to inspect its lunar telescope housing units to determine implantation techniques. With this knowledge, Imbrium's own telescopes can be set up and calibrated for permanent use.

By monitoring the near and wide-angle television circuits on the console, the Imbrium Base crew will be able to see what is happening in a dozen different places. They will see the plot boards inside L-4, obtain an exceptionally wide view of the Earth, see the area around their own Shelter, see two different sections of Station SS-9, watch the approach areas leading from Archimedes Base and monitor the sections within their own Shelter.

In an hour-long conference poring over charts, the three crewmen will begin to plot the positioning of the soon-to-arrive additional Base Shelters and the main Baseline Station Building. There are many things to be considered in addition, including the placement of two astronomical telescopes and a solar telescope, a place for the central landing field, location of the main nuclear power plant, shelter housing for the tractors, Rovers and Lunar Buses. Between the Base and the LaPlace Promontory, seismic soundings will have to be taken quickly to determine a location for all the future underground storage, operations and technical laboratories that will make up an enormous sub-surface city for several hundred people. Perhaps, some day, the Imbrium population will grow to several thousand, like Archimedes.

As on Earth, the men will eat three basic meals a day plus two energy snacks between meals. The food for the most part will be cooked instantaneously inside an electronic stove compartment. Many liquid drinks will be transported in the form of powder to be mixed with water. The lunar explorers will eat much the same foods as are eaten on Earth, but they will have been specially wrapped in space-saving packages. Dishes, cups and utensils will be made of hardened paper for easy disposal; many foods will be eaten right out of the package.

After supper, the explorers will return to their work stations to make final preparations for morning arrivals. The film will arrive from Archimedes by a special lunar "sled" a one-man manoeuvring unit consisting of seat, storage compartment and propulsion unit, all attached to a bare frame. It will be the most common type of man-transportation system on the Moon.

The use of the "thumper," a tubular, cartridge-firing device to create small seismic waves on the lunar surface, is demonstrated here by Joseph Engle, who was back-up pilot for Apollo 14.

53

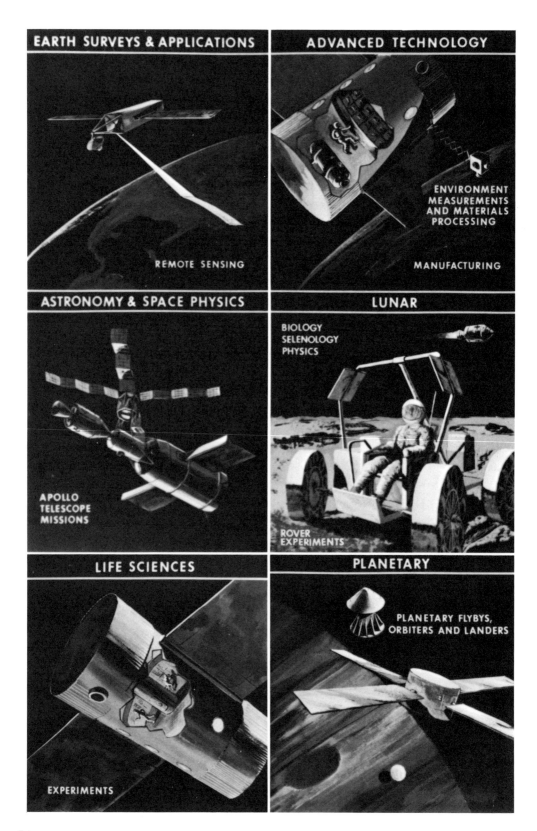

EARTH SURVEYS & APPLICATIONS

REMOTE SENSING

ADVANCED TECHNOLOGY

ENVIRONMENT
MEASUREMENTS
AND MATERIALS
PROCESSING

MANUFACTURING

ASTRONOMY & SPACE PHYSICS

APOLLO
TELESCOPE
MISSIONS

LUNAR

BIOLOGY
SELENOLOGY
PHYSICS

ROVER
EXPERIMENTS

LIFE SCIENCES

EXPERIMENTS

PLANETARY

PLANETARY FLYBYS,
ORBITERS AND LANDERS

The Base crew members will have an opportunity to visit for a few minutes with the messenger from Archimedes. After he has gone, the crew will monitor all the instrument devices and make a final check of all on-board systems. The men will then sit down to watch the film; it will be their only chance because the work they will have to do in the next several weeks will occupy all their time.

The astronauts will go to sleep by the clock, according to sleep periods. At 10 o'clock (2200), two of the team members will go to sleep, while the third will begin the first watch for the "night." Each of the three men will have one four-hour watch each in every 12-hour "night," and each will thus have eight hours of sleep. The lunar "day" of 14 days duration has just begun, so for the Moon explorers there will be no darkness until 14 days later.

Exploring the Heavens by Moonscope

Astronomical, planetary and solar telescopes will be exceedingly important instruments in the continuing conquest of the universe. Some telescopes are now being designed to orbit the Earth as instrumentation modules. Totally unmanned, they are to be guided and operated automatically from a Space Station or from the Earth, and their primary work will be accomplished through photography. Film packs will be changed intermittently. The taking of pictures will be monitored by a technician who has instant close-up television views of the interior of the module to see that the mechanism is working properly.

After the first 100-inch telescopes are placed on the Moon and put into operation, space scientists believe that man's view of the universe then will be expanded at least one-hundred-fold. Once outside of the Earth's protective blanket of clouds and gases which we call the atmosphere, "seeing" out into space becomes totally unrestricted. Earth-based telescopes, for instance, when focussing on the planet Venus must actually see through two distinct layers of atmosphere—the Earth's and the one on Venus. Seeing should be many times clearer, then, when one of these atmospheric layers is avoided.

In space, stars do not twinkle; they burn with a steady light. We see them twinkle on Earth because of our atmosphere. For the same reason, astronomers can now only partially measure a planet or star by spectro-analysis— that is, studying the light wavelengths emitted by a star. But with atmosphere eliminated, such measurement will become much more exact and the astronauts will come much closer to exactness in studying objects out in space.

Moon-based telescopes will first be delivered "naked" with a bare minimum

(Opposite page) In the near future, NASA has plans to work in these ways.

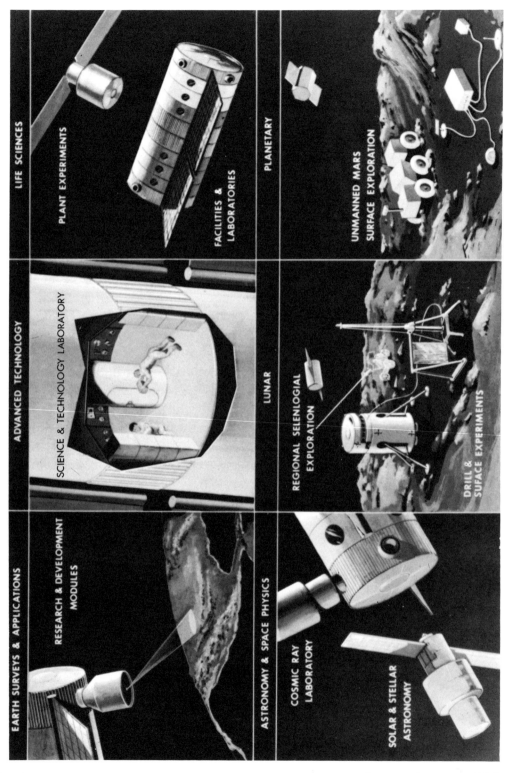

In the late 1970's, as the hardware capability of space science advances, NASA has plans to work in the above ways.

of protective covering. Once they have been installed, subsequent Shuttle flights will deliver "shelter" housings that can be built around them and in time provide a "shirt-sleeve" environment so scientists can work comfortably inside an air-tight observatory.

Scientists are vitally interested in the strange phenomena that continually occur on or around the Sun. Solar telescopes on the Moon will give astronauts a much better chance of studying the Sun's seething surface, its chromosphere, the astonishing prominences that sometimes shoot out hundreds of miles from its surface, and the nature and movement of sunspots. Because of such study, scientists will undoubtedly discover new ways not only of using the Sun's energy and radiation, but also new ways to protect ourselves from its harmful effects. Our lives on Earth will certainly be changed by much of what they learn.

By the time the mythical Mare Imbrium Lunar Base is established in 1980, scientific and photographic vehicles will probably have travelled to Mars, Venus, Jupiter and Saturn. Scientists will have close-up pictures of thee, planets to study, as well as measurements of their chemical composition. Several unmanned probes will also have landed on the surface of Mars especially, in preparation for manned exploration later in the 1980's, according to present plan. Moon-based telescopes will allow scientists to study the surface of Mars on a sustained basis to observe changes and other phenomena that might occur, such as the immense "dust storms" encountered by the Mariner spacecraft in 1971.

Only by observation on a constant schedule can scientists ever really learn about another planet sufficiently to get a true idea of it. Looking through a telescope for only a few minutes at a time is like coming into a theatre in the middle of the movie. The longer we stay, the more we begin to understand the story being told on the screen, and then the more we begin to understand the many little details that go to make up the whole movie. The same thing applies to astronomical observation—it takes time to develop a true understanding of the object being studied. And determined dedication as well.

Living and Working on the Moon

In the long-term plan for the exploration of the Moon, it is important for man to have the capability of living there for long periods. It is expected that the little lunar bases that are established in the 1980's will grow to villages, then towns, and finally into huge cities by the 21st century. The time may come when people are born and die on the Moon, perhaps even without ever visiting another body in space. A new type of society and culture could develop, based on the restrictions and advantages of a wholly new kind of environment. To really put the Moon to work for us, men must be able to live there for decades with relative freedom of movement. This entails family life that is peculiarly adapted to the Moon.

For space science, the 1960's was a period of testing men and machines to obtain a certain level of capability for both. Scientists learned what the space and lunar environments were all about, and designed vehicles to move men and instruments about on a limited scale.

The decade of the 1970's will be a similar period in which scientists perfect machinery and instruments and learn in greater detail how to prepare man for longer survival times in space and on the Moon. In the 1980's, they will continue to develop instruments and machines, and begin to study the Moon in precise detail, hopefully by spending large amounts of time there. At the same time, scientists will also begin to concentrate some investigations on the nearby planets, especially Mars, and perhaps land teams of explorers on them.

All the while, scientists will be preparing for the day when men can stay on the Moon indefinitely. By the time the decade of the 1990's arrives, the lunar bases will possibly have been expanded greatly and scientists will have solved most of the basic problems. By the turn of the century, and the year 2000, men should be ready to build Moon cities and begin permanent colonization that will evolve into a real lunar culture.

Looking toward the future, even scientists can only guess what is to come and try to plan realistically for expected events. But their guesses must be supported by a certain amount of known information—an amount that grows in geometric ratio with each hour men spend on the Moon. From the experiences of the astronauts in the Apollo program, scientists believe it is possible to build either an underground city or a heavily protected surface city on the Moon. Perhaps the metropolis will be a combination of both. Everything will depend upon what is discovered on the Moon in the 1970's and 1980's.

Scientists will have to study the structure and composition of the Moon in detail to determine such specifics as the frequency and extent of lunar volcanic activity; the degree of hardness or hollowness of the Moon's interior; the possibility of growing things on the Moon, perhaps even the possibility of constructing an atmosphere there similar to Earth's; the nature and amount of harmful radiation falling on the Moon; the likelihood of using lunar soil to construct buildings, roads, bridges and even highways. In short, they must find out how different the Moon is from the Earth, and if decidedly different, how to cope with these differences and turn them to man's advantage.

Before the year 2000, the plan is for men to be living and working on the Moon. Life will not be easy because much of it will be determined by the use of artificial devices and systems to sustain human life. The astronauts will have to carry the Earth environment with them, meaning life-support materials. They will either have to learn how to walk differently or else how to weight themselves down so that they can function normally to perform normal tasks. They will have to think constantly about protection—from the Sun, from extremes of temperature, from lack of oxygen, from debris falling upon them, and from accidental death due to a sudden volcanic eruption or earthquake on the Moon. They will have to learn to be Moon people.

Once they have found a means of adapting to the Moon, the next important step is finding out how to put the Moon to work. Can man profit from the minerals and natural formations found there? What new chemicals or minerals will be found, and how will they change our lives both on Earth and on the Moon? How costly will it be to have to transport all the materials from the Earth to the Moon, and will this cost be worth the end results?

An Apollo program director stated NASA's dilemma quite clearly when he said: "Landing a man on the Moon has prompted a hundred times more questions about the nature of the Moon than we ever originally had. Every time we send a team up there, they come back with more questions to be answered and more problems to be solved. It's going to be like this for a long time to come, until we learn what kind of a place the Moon really is."

How long can a man psychologically and physically withstand living and working on the Moon in a Shelter or Lunar Base situation? How much protection can scientists and engineers give him today, and how quickly can this protection be increased or decreased in the future? What unknown effects upon the human body, such as maladies in vision, hearing, muscle flexion and body balance, will occur to men living on the Moon for long periods of time? The questions are unending, but they must all be answered. Time is against us; we are eager to learn and anxious to explore, and sometimes impatient out of sheer curiosity. Man's mind works faster than his hands.

The large Lunar Base of the 1990's is expected to be a busy scene. By then, the type of orbiting Space Station discussed earlier will hopefully have become a way-station on the highway between Earth and Moon. The space suit will have been modified many times into a more compact garment in which it is easier to move about. Trucks, buses and other vehicles will possibly be rolling across the lunar surface carrying precious cargoes of men and materials. They will have to travel on designed roadways, and be powered by electronic and nuclear energy units. Astronauts and scientists are expected to fly across the Moon by means of jet-propulsion Manoeuvring Units that will whisk them up into space in open-air sleds. The 1990's Moon Base, if it comes into being, will be the scene of constant excitement over new discoveries and there will be an unbridled spirit of adventure surrounding new explorations. What the astronauts learn and the materials they gather from the Moon will help build a new future for man in space.

2. A VISIT TO MARS

Mars has been the subject of continuous and concentrated study for centuries. It was not until 1877, however, when Giovanni Schiaparelli reported seeing *canali* on Mars that intense public interest was focussed on the planet. The word *canali* is an Italian word meaning "channels" or "canals" and many scientists soon began to wonder if the channels or canals might have been built by intelligent beings. The prospect of life on another planet intrigued all of mankind. Not long afterwards, stories of "Martians" and space travel to Mars became a highly popular subject. Recent studies of Mars by several Mariner spacecraft have disclosed the surface to be much like that of our Moon—and dashed, at least for the moment, any hopes of finding a higher order of life there.

Still, science is especially interested in Mars—not because it is like the Earth, but rather because it is more like the Earth than are any of the other planets. The Mariner 4 photographic spacecraft in 1964 took 22 pictures of the Martian surface during one sweep past, in what space scientists call a "flyby" mission. One frame in particular, No. 11, was of extreme interest to researchers at Pasadena's Jet Propulsion Laboratory at the California Institute of Technology, which had responsibility for tracking and data gathering. The frame showed a group of several large craters of the same appearance as those the Ranger spacecraft had found on the Moon. That picture was

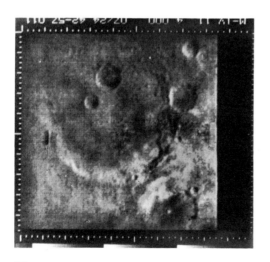

This is Mariner 4's photograph No. 11 which startled the scientific community when it was received in 1965 by television from the spacecraft at the Jet Propulsion Laboratory in Pasadena, California. It brought about a significant change in planetary exploration, because it showed Mars' craters for the first time, and the craters looked remarkably like those on the Moon, giving the first indication that Mars might be lifeless.

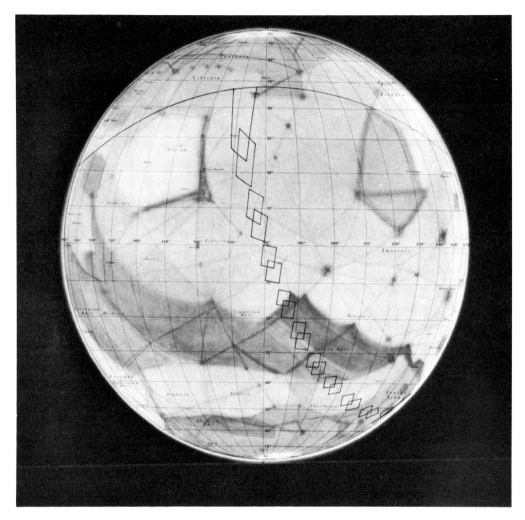

Mariner 4 took a sequence of 22 photographs, which were later charted like this on the map of Mars.

acclaimed as one of the pictures of the century because it told in one concise photograph nearly the whole story of Mars as probably a lifeless planet.

Why does anyone want to go to Mars? There are a few highly important reasons. For one thing, it would be the first step out of our own planet's influence. Also, men would actually set foot upon a body whirling about in space not subject to the Earth's movement. The mastery of technology needed to land on Mars will allow men to go to other planets as well. In effect, then, Mars will be the testing ground for men, machines and systems required to make space travel a reality. If men cannot conquer that technology, then all hope of ever exploring space might as well be abandoned.

What scientists learn about Mars will help unravel the remaining mysteries of our Solar System—how it began, when it was created, what it is made of.

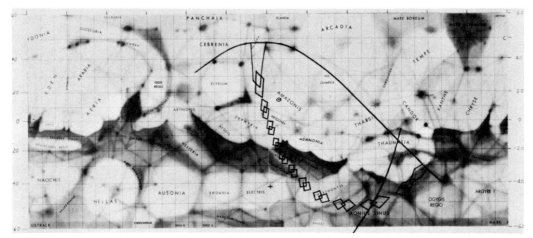

Projected onto a standard Mercator map of Mars, the sequence of photographs taken by Mariner 4 looked like this.

If Earth creatures are peculiarly fortunate to inhabit the only inhabitable planet in our Solar System, is it still possible to renovate another planet or to learn how to adapt to the environment of another planet? A journey to Mars will tell us if men can ever live there and survive.

Scientists need to know what life forms exist on Mars, if any; they will always find a way to make use of what they find, but how difficult and how costly will it be to do so? If extraterrestrial life is discovered on Mars, it will profoundly affect our concept of the universe and greatly change our outlook. Perhaps an exchange of life forms is possible between the planets. If so, the potential of Mars as a useful planet is incalculable.

Mars can very well become a permanent "space station" in our Solar System—a jumping-off point to other planets. It could become a springboard to places beyond our Solar System to reach other bodies and make new discoveries in the swarm of stars and gases that we call our galaxy. A permanent human colony on Mars in the first quarter of the 21st century will be of inestimable value in expanding our studies of the universe.

Four Mariner spacecraft have been to Mars: Mariner 4 in 1964, Mariners 6 and 7 in 1969, and Mariner 9 in 1971-72. Each mission provided a different view of the planet, and all contributed collectively to increase our understanding of just what kind of a place Mars is. Mariner 4 showed us a planet pockmarked with many different kinds of craters; Mariners 6 and 7 disclosed a rugged, abused crust of chaotic and disturbed appearance suggesting massive quakes, crumbling and twisted upheavals, and large, dry plains; Mariner 9 found enormous dust storms sweeping across a barren, lifeless landscape and also showed what one of Mars' moons looks like. In all, scientists now believe Mars to be unique in the Solar System, and somewhat disappointing as a platform for life as we know it to be on Earth. But they must learn more.

Project Viking

Continued study of Mars will have to be carried out extensively before any humans are permitted to travel there. Scientists do not yet know enough about the planet to be able to assure the astronauts' total safety. This investigation is expected to be accomplished by a Mariner vehicle placed in Mars orbit for continuous photography, as was used by Mariner 9, and then by a Viking spacecraft for both orbiting and soft landings on the Mars terrain, in 1975 or mid-1976.

The Viking craft is actually a double spacecraft, a combination of orbiter and lander. One half of the vehicle will remain in orbit, setting loose a lander craft to be parachuted to the planet's surface. The lander will carry experiments right down onto the Martian landscape, similar to those conducted by the Moon-probe Surveyor. Mechanical arms will retrieve and manipulate the soil and rocks. Biochemical experiments will then test the gathered material and radio the results back to Earth.

A scale model of the NASA Viking spacecraft in simulated flight. It has two parts: an Orbiter section which will make investigations from Martian orbit, and a Lander section that will explore the planet's surface and sample the soil and air.

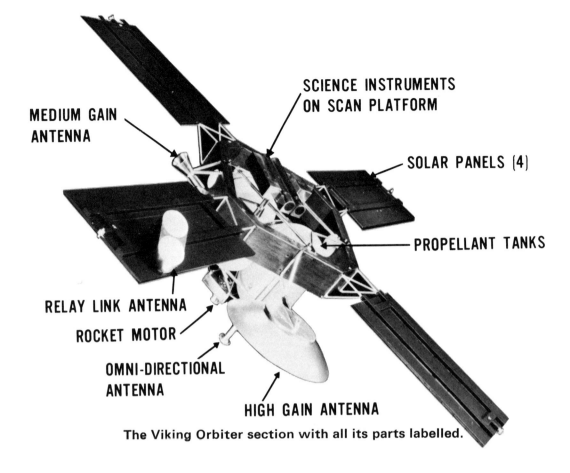

MEDIUM GAIN
ANTENNA

SCIENCE INSTRUMENTS
ON SCAN PLATFORM

SOLAR PANELS (4)

PROPELLANT TANKS

RELAY LINK ANTENNA

ROCKET MOTOR

OMNI-DIRECTIONAL
ANTENNA

HIGH GAIN ANTENNA

The Viking Orbiter section with all its parts labelled.

The Viking program, now in the planning stage, is an outgrowth of several mechanical concepts that have already been used successfully in space exploration. It draws from the Apollo Command Module and Lunar Module concept; it is designed much like the Mariner craft except in an expanded version; and its lander portion was designed after the basic Surveyor type of craft. Because of its double purpose, all these concepts have been rolled into one design.

The Viking mission profile calls for a number of other changes, as follows: Viking will need three times as much propulsion capacity as the Mariner 1971 craft because of the necessity for orbital Mars insertion and the size of the lander. Therefore it will have to be launched by a Titan III Centaur launch rocket. Viking will have six solar cell panels instead of four. The battery capacity will be increased for higher electrical demands. The equipment section will require 16 compartments instead of Mariner's eight, because of the increased amount of experiments and the considerably more complicated manoeuvres required of Viking. Finally, a new type of receiver has been designed to pick up the lander's transmissions and relay them to Earth. In all, Viking will be a far different craft from Mariner.

Once Viking is in Mars orbit, a "bioshield" used to protect it from space debris will be jettisoned. Then the lander portion of the vehicle will separate from the mother craft and de-orbit towards the surface. At 18,000 feet above the landscape, a large parachute will blossom out, and about 15 seconds later the protective "aeroshield" enclosing the sterile lander will be jettisoned leaving the lander free to touch down. At 4,800 feet, braking rockets aboard the lander will begin to slow the craft. Then, at 3,900 feet above the Martian surface, the parachute will be let loose and the lander will be further slowed by retro-rockets. Special shock-absorbing cushions will take up the impact of landing.

The Viking lander is a triangular box containing specific scientific equipment and experimentation missions. The request for experiments to be carried aboard Viking numbered 165 proposals; only 25 were finally selected for planning. All its equipment must be designed into the lander at the time it is being built. Some of the experiments include: measuring composition of the upper atmosphere, ion and electron densities, and energy distribution; measuring density, pressure and temperature distribution in the lower atmosphere; measuring atmospheric pressure and temperature at the surface; measuring wind speed, direction, humidity, seismic activity, abundance of water distribution in the atmosphere, and variation of surface temperatures

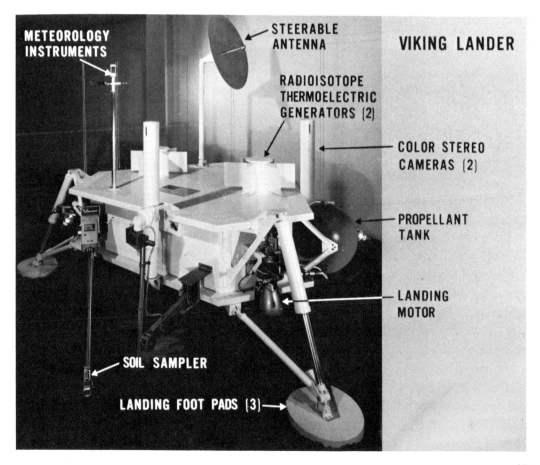

METEOROLOGY INSTRUMENTS

STEERABLE ANTENNA

VIKING LANDER

RADIOISOTOPE THERMOELECTRIC GENERATORS (2)

COLOR STEREO CAMERAS (2)

PROPELLANT TANK

LANDING MOTOR

SOIL SAMPLER

LANDING FOOT PADS (3)→

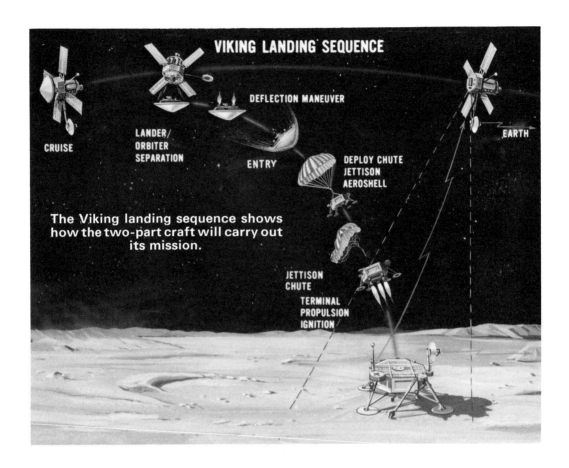

VIKING LANDING SEQUENCE

DEFLECTION MANEUVER

CRUISE

LANDER/
ORBITER
SEPARATION

ENTRY

EARTH

DEPLOY CHUTE
JETTISON
AEROSHELL

JETTISON
CHUTE

TERMINAL
PROPULSION
IGNITION

The Viking landing sequence shows
how the two-part craft will carry out
its mission.

and thermal balance near or at the surface; detecting photosynthesis and respiratory fixation of isotopic carbon dioxide by soil sample; detecting changes in gas composition over incubated soil samples.

Two Viking missions are tentatively scheduled for 1975. Each lander portion is designed for three months of continuous operation after touchdown. At that time (Earth summertime) Mars will be 52,400,000 miles from Earth, and it will take nearly a year for Viking to reach the planet. The orbiter portion of Viking will actually scan the Mars landscape and select the most likely site on which to set the lander portion down. In order to reach Mars at just the right place, Viking will be placed in an interplanetary transfer ellipse with an azimuth of 90° to 108°. Three separate mid-course corrections will be made during the 12-month travel time to Mars. Once the lander has touched down, it will become a highly significant scientific outpost on Mars. Then scientists on Earth will begin to know what kind of a planet they are dealing with.

Scientists have no illusions about the Viking missions. Touching a planet at only two of its points leaves an immense area of its surface untapped. Such a mission concept can be compared to scientists from Mars launching a Viking spacecraft that touches down on Earth on the Sahara Desert, and following it with another that lands in the Florida Everglades. Trying to make accurate scientific assumptions from such missions will be difficult indeed. At least, though, scientists already have enough view of Mars from Mariner photos to know what most of it is like. Viking will help to shrink our abundant ignorance.

A Mars Landing Team

Understanding of Mars has changed drastically since the flight of Mariner 4 in 1964. Scientists no longer have fantasies of lush Martian vegetation fed by water passed through intricate and extensive canals built by a superior race of beings who have tried unsuccessfully to contact Earth across space. Instead, they have discovered an apparently lifeless, dry and hostile planet racked occasionally by raging dust storms and violently abused by crashing meteorites and internal upheavals. But the romance of Mars still beckons scientists—the need to know drives them on.

In NASA's long-range planning, scientists are being set to work to devise a means of landing a team of explorers on Mars, perhaps in the 1980's. The team will carry its own life-support supply because the Martian atmosphere is abundant in carbon dioxide which, on Earth, is the waste portion of man's breathing. (We inhale oxygen and exhale carbon dioxide.) Stable water

 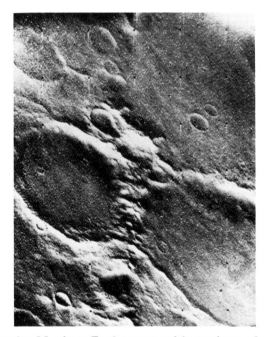

Mars' south Polar Cap region (left), taken by Mariner 7, shows a wide variety of crater sizes and blotchy features. An enlarged photo of a "giant footprint" crater (right) shows an unusual formation.

exists on Mars only in the form of vapor or ice, and although there is water vapor in the Martian atmosphere, there is not enough to provide liquid water in quantity. As a planet, then, Mars is an exceedingly harsh environment where only the lowest forms of life can survive if indeed they survive at all. Mars' atmosphere is extremely thin compared to Earth's, but it extends for a far greater distance. Therefore, there is little cloudiness on Mars, although Mariners' investigations have detected a few ill-defined areas of isolated clouds or fog in the polar-cap region.

In general terms, the machines and systems developed for use on the Moon could very well serve to permit extensive exploration of Mars. The Martian terrain is more like the Moon's than the Earth's, which will be a definite aid in adapting lunar vehicles and shelters for use on Mars. Protection of human life, however, will be a far more important objective.

Surface temperatures vary from place to place on Mars, but daytime

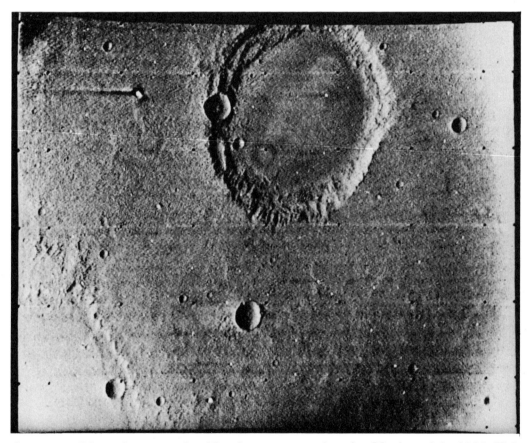

A truly striking close-up of a Martian crater, taken by Mariner 6 in 1969. This narrow-angle picture shows an area 63 miles east to west and 48 miles north to south. The large crater is about 24 miles across. It shows several slump terraces, especially on the west inner wall; both are features typical of some of the larger craters on the Moon. The gullies and troughs round the crater and elsewhere are also similar to Moon features.

MARS INITIAL LANDING

This artist's painting depicts a Mars landing team collecting rock samples on their first exploratory attempt. A Martian Rover-type vehicle similar to the one used on the Moon and surface-sensing instruments are shown in the background.

temperatures near the equator seem to be about 62° F (16° C) at noon and about –45° F (–42° C) at the polar-cap edge. At night, the equatorial temperature drops to –100° F (–73° C). The actual polar-cap temperature was found to be about –193° F (–185° C).

Mariner 6 and 7 television pictures indicated very little seasonal darkening of the Martian surface. The supposed "canals" were found to be linear alignments or long strings of craters with dark floors. Mariner 9 in 1971 disclosed large areas of surface features looking as though Mars had been racked at one time by immense internal convulsions that resulted in surface upheavals.

We must be extremely careful not to misinterpret the findings of the Mariner flights in telling us what Mars is all about. Scientists now believe, though, that Mars' evolutionary development is quite different from the Moon's history, and decidedly different from Earth's. Mars may be at an evolutionary development stage that was experienced in some respects by the Earth long, long ago. Scientists cannot be certain of this until actual soil samples are tested and other features examined up close. The mysteries of Mars cannot be solved until man journeys to the planet.

A Mars astronaut team will have to spend about 8 to 10 months in interplanetary travel from their launch site on Earth to final touchdown on Mars. In doing so, the team would make maximum use of manned Earth-orbital and Lunar-operating experiences. A Space Station Module attached to the Mars spacecraft would house the team during the flight to Mars and on the return flight to Earth, scientists now calculate. Lunar exploration methods will be followed for Mars surface operations. In essence, then, the Mars exploration project will be an extended project of the type of journey to the Moon and back already experienced by numerous Apollo Moon teams.

Because of the great travel time to Mars, the astronauts will have to be sustained for a long period, requiring more space aboard the spacecraft for storage of food, navigational and operational instruments, and for waste management. The spacecraft will require larger booster rocket power for the long voyage and to put the heavier payload into interplanetary orbit. Double and sometimes triple safety features will be built into all the project's systems. In short, the spacecraft going to Mars will have to be bigger and therefore heavier.

Upon reaching the vicinity of Mars, the spacecraft will enter a Mars orbital sequence and remain there while procedures are set in motion for separation of the landing module at the pre-selected site. At the right moment, the Mars surface craft will disconnect and begin the drop to the surface, just as the Apollo landing module set down on the lunar surface. Using a retro-rocket braking system, the Mars Excursion Module will be slowed down for the landing, finally settling to rest. Men from Earth will have journeyed to a far

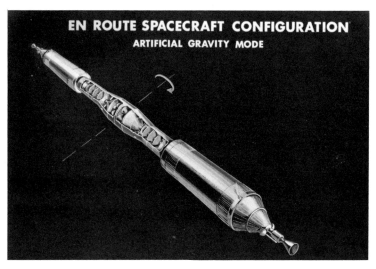

EN ROUTE SPACECRAFT CONFIGURATION
ARTIFICIAL GRAVITY MODE

Two spacecraft en route to Mars could be coupled together as shown in this illustration. Gravity during the journey would be supplied to the explorers by rotating the entire configuration end-for-end.

A control center like this one in Pasadena, California, which participated in the Apollo flights, will be needed to handle spacecraft missions to Mars and other planets. The consoles continually follow the status of the mission. This laboratory, when fully operational, can control two simultaneous command missions to interplanetary space, and monitor a third.

and distant planet. Meanwhile, the Mars Command Module, or "mother craft," will continue to circle the planet awaiting the return of the exploration team.

The first explorations of the Martian surface will be much like those made on the Moon by the Apollo astronauts. There will be a great deal of work to do. Instruments will be set up for recording Martian phenomena—seismometer, magnetometer, wind vanes, temperature gauges, communications antennae, television cameras, and solar-sensing instruments. Perhaps even on this first flight a Rover type of vehicle will be carried for short-distance investigation.

The astronaut on Mars will weigh about one third of what he weighs on Earth, which could very well be a serious problem because of the wind speeds on Mars that evidently come up suddenly and with considerable force. Special suits will provide protection from the Sun's rays as well as the lethal

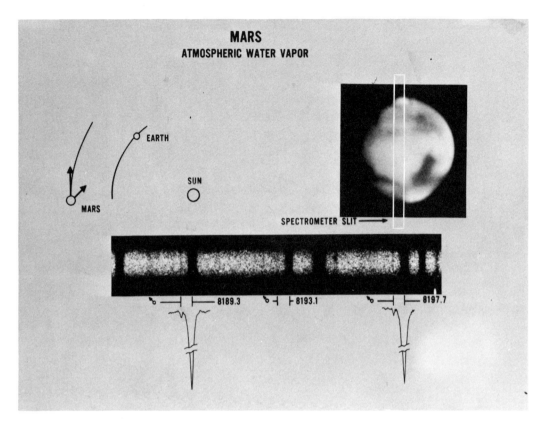

MARS
ATMOSPHERIC WATER VAPOR

EARTH

SUN

MARS

SPECTROMETER SLIT ⟶

8189.3   8193.1   8197.7

Spectrometer analysis of Mars' atmosphere across the center of the planet reveals little or no water content as measured from Earth-based instruments. The Viking Lander will give space scientists an on-the-spot analysis and provide a final answer to the questions about the Martian environment.

ground atmosphere of carbon dioxide and other harmful, toxic gases. Surface samples will have to be gathered, including rocks, soil, any possible examples of living organisms, and certainly any evidence of free liquids.

The Mars Excursion team will be able to remain on the Martian surface for only a short time—perhaps just a few days. That will be sufficient time to conduct all the experimentation and investigation necessary for the initial Mars encounter. During that time, the team will have to carry out normal human functions as well—eating, sleeping, recording reports and impressions, relaxing after hours of intense excitement in discovering new things. At times, the crew will mount the Mars Rover vehicle depending upon how clear the air is at the surface of the planet. With extreme care, they will "drive" their car to certain points of interest for examination, returning after short travel times. It will not be a good idea to get too far from the Excursion Module in case of impending disaster.

After the exploration period is ended, the Mars Excursion Module will launch itself up off the landscape and rendezvous with the Command Module already in Mars orbit. Once the crew is safely docked, the Mars Exploration vehicle will swing out of orbit and head for the Earth. The long trip back will this time be filled with the many chores of investigating the region through which the spacecraft is passing. The astronauts/scientists will conduct photographic and spectrographic studies of celestial objects, perform their own medical and biological experiments and monitor the experiments set in motion when they first left Earth.

A great deal of the information needed before the astronauts can undertake a voyage to Mars is yet to be gathered. Specific studies to be carried out on board Space Stations in Earth and Lunar orbits will contribute substantially to the design and equipping of a Mars Exploration spacecraft. Scientists are greatly concerned over the effects of 8 to 10 months of weightlessness on the way to Mars, and the additional 8 to 10 months required for the return. Artificial exercise periods will have to be employed to keep the astronauts in good physical condition; visual and auditory tests and exercises will be carried out during both legs of the journey.

Waste management will be a constant concern. By the middle of the 1980's, scientists will have found a way to disintegrate or substantially reduce the size of waste materials so they won't take up needed storage space. Packaging of food and instrument containers will be critical to prevent an overabundance of throw-away cartons. Human waste is still under intensive study by scientists seeking to find ways to re-cycle urine into usable washing or maintenance water, and to reduce the size of fecal deposits into more manageable packages. Since much equipment will be left on the Martian surface for monitoring by Earth-based instruments, more storage space will be available on the return trip. Some of this storage space, however, will be taken up with samples of Martian rocks and soil.

Space and Time

In order to make interplanetary travel a reality, scientists must solve the two most important problems presenting barriers to success—distance and time. Signals from Mariner Orbiters and Flybys sent from the vicinity of Mars require about 6½ minutes to cover the distance between Earth and Mars. An astronaut standing on the surface of Mars asking a question of Houston Mission Control will have to wait 13 minutes for a reply, using conventional radio signals. Communication between the two planets will be slow indeed.

From the very start of the space program, studies have been undertaken with laser beams to determine their usefulness in communicating. Astronauts on Mars will on the average be approximately 50 million miles from Earth—a distance difficult for Earthbound man to comprehend since we do not normally deal in such extreme quantities. To cross that great expanse quickly will

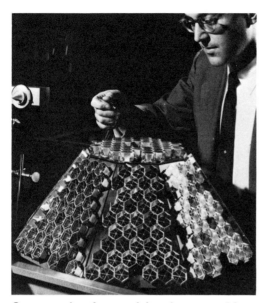

Communications with a base on Mars might be carried by laser beams, rather than radio. Here is an eight-sided pyramid mounted with 360 laser reflectors. The reflectors are cube-cornered so that light from a ground-based laser transmitter can strike them from almost any angle and be returned to its source. Artificial satellites now carry such pyramids.

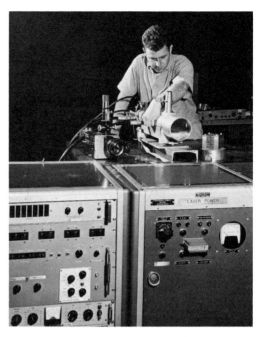

If a laser beam reflector were to orbit Mars, this sampling unit would be used to trigger a device to measure the time required for the laser beam to travel to the orbiting reflector and return. It is now used with laser beams to artificial Earth satellites.

require a signal that can travel at least with the speed of light, or about 186,282 miles per second.

A single laser beam can carry many telephone calls and television signals all at one time. Successful studies have already been conducted between ground stations and moving aircraft. A laser beam of cohesive light travels in a straight line, but it may suffer interference, and be bent or broken while travelling from Mars to Earth by passing through two planetary atmospheres and the unknown contents of interplanetary space. Much more work needs to be done in this field before the laser beam can be adapted to such long-range communications. Perhaps the answer to interplanetary communications can be solved by a series of relay stations that pick up and re-broadcast or re-direct laser beams.

NASA has made a number of preliminary investigations of nuclear power and its adaptability to space flight. Most of these programs have been temporarily suspended, but nearly all of them were carried far enough in the work-up stages to make engineers realize their usefulness. Two radio-isotope generators are already being used in space: SNAP-19 (Systems for

Nuclear Auxiliary Power), producing power for NASA's Nimbus III weather satellite, and SNAP-27 left on the Moon by the Apollo 12 crew to power the equipment implanted at their landing site. Both are low-power generating sources. Other components of nuclear power sources have been used in other satellites with encouarging results. Most important now is the development of a nuclear engine capable of faster travel and of lifting heavier loads.

A nuclear engine project called NERVA (Nuclear Energy for Rocket Vehicle Application) has long been in a developmental stage and was ground-tested in February, 1966, using liquid hydrogen. The engine runs in cycles, providing over-all high thrust intervals, and is capable of generating great speed and of lifting quite heavy payloads. NASA hopes to use this type of nuclear engine in the Space Shuttle Craft, and if successful, adapt it to use with the Mars Excursion system of the 1980's.

Learning to Be a Martian

A 200-pound man from Earth would weigh roughly 78 pounds on Mars. A Martian-born creature, in other ways too, would be far different in appearance and life form from anything Earth man is accustomed to seeing. Mars man would primarily be a carbon dioxide-breathing creature with a thin, absorptive membrane located in a protected place on his body to synthesize a maximum amount of moisture. He would sustain himself on a diet of algae and primitive growth forms and be protected by a heavy, rough skin covering to protect him from temperature changes and from the rugged Martian landscape of rocks, trenches and rock-formed peaks. His mouth would be quite large, protruding away from his skull to enable him to get at tiny food forms.

A Martian's eyes would have to be large, possibly employing a nictitating membrane that covers the eyeball not only for protection against sudden storms and temperature drops, but to enable him to see sufficiently amidst the ground atmosphere haze and fog banks. His ears also would be large—the ground atmosphere would inhibit the travel of sound waves which would be dulled and muted by the Martian environment. These ears would probably be rough-skinned and protected somewhat by hair. A Martian would have little need for a nose, which might consist merely of a small nasal opening flat against his face or as part of his absorptive membrane.

To be functionally mobile on the Martian landscape, the creature would have to be built close to the ground—perhaps as small as 2 or 3 feet high. While his body would have to be fairly fat and round to store large amounts of energy and food, his arms would have to be rather long to facilitate climbing. His legs, too, would have to be more than stubby protrusions—perhaps 3 or 4 in number to maintain balance of a cumbersome body, and tough but slender to facilitate climbing and walking. The creature would not be built for speed since there is little to run to or from on the bleak landscape.

A creature like the one just described is based upon many of the facts we know about the Martian environment. It assumes life on Mars could include a moving, thinking, rational creature who in a sense is master of his own destiny. In many respects, the creature would be at a very low evolutionary stage measured by our scale of evolutionary development. According to modern anthropologists, Earth man passed this stage some 3 to 4 million years ago. But the example will serve to indicate physical development of a creature likely to survive on Mars if indeed creatures actually did or do live there. No investigations of Mars have ever found evidence of men or any form of higher life on the planet.

Earth man has none of the faculties of the creature just described, and so the astronaut arriving there would have to compensate for these deficiencies and make the best possible use of his higher evolutionary state. A protective space suit, back-pack containing life support and communications equipment, and instruments to do his work will enable the astronaut from Earth to survive his experience on Mars. But there are other differences and similarities to get used to.

In volume, Mars is much smaller than Earth—in fact, only half the size. A Martian day is 24 hours 37 minutes long, and the Mars year lasts 668 days compared to Earth's 365. Mars has two natural satellites, the moons Deimos and Phobos, which are quite tiny and of little use physically as manned stations in Mars orbit. Mars changes the tilt of its axis to provide annual seasons, but these are usually little more than changes in temperature and surface wind activity, because there appears to be little or no vegetation on the planet. The polar ice cap visibly changes size during the year and consists mainly of ice with frost at its fringes.

This Mars mosaic is made up of four wide-angle photos taken by Mariner 6. By composite photo-spreads such as this, astronauts and scientists can get a better understanding of the planet's surface. This mosaic covers an area 450 by 2,500 miles. The black spot on each photo is a blemish on the TV camera.

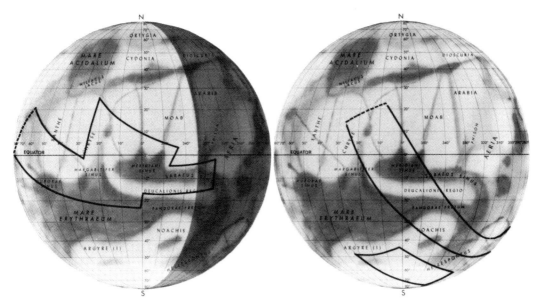

In 1969, Mariner 6 made a flyby across the equator of Mars, and a few days later, Mariner 7 made a polar flyby, as shown here. Little by little, the entire surface of the planet is being photographed.

Preliminary reports from the Mariner flights to Mars indicate an abundance of silica in the upper atmosphere, decreasing in amount down toward the planet's surface. The lack of sufficient quantities of nitrogen and helium to support human life make Mars an unlikely candidate for human habitation without oxygen tanks and space suits. In fact, Mars is not the generously hospitable planet we once believed and hoped it would be. Learning to be a Martian, therefore, will be a difficult task.

Explorers to Mars can expect a ground covering similar to what the astronauts found on the Moon, and astronauts will have to learn to wade through it at one third their normal weight. "Seeing" will probably be somewhat difficult on Mars because of ground level disturbances and debris-tossing winds. Sudden temperature drops at night will be hard on equipment and its mobility, and they will have to be taken into consideration by the engineers who design such equipment.

The list of questions to be answered about Mars is long and detailed, but eventually they must all be answered. Some of the most obvious are:

How was the chaotic Martian terrain created?

What caused the two distinct types of craters, and why are they different?

How did the wide stretches of featureless landscape escape meteorite bombardment?

What caused the Hellas region (300,000 square miles) to change from bright reflectance to a dark appearance in 1954?

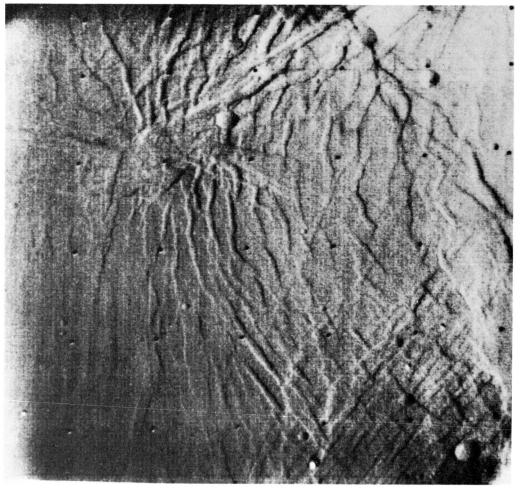

Unlike any other view of Mars, this photo was taken by Mariner 9 on its 67th orbit in late 1971. Three weeks earlier this plateau was hidden by a great dust storm. The appearance of the terrain indicates to geologists that it is relatively young and may have been covered by volcanic deposits and be subject to faults or cracks in the surface.

How were the apparent straight lines of the Martian surface created?

What causes the "waves of darkening" that suddenly sweep toward Mars' equator in the summertime?

What caused the great yellow clouds that suddenly appeared, as in 1877, 1909, 1922 and 1956?

Is there life on Mars? What kind of life is it?

The first Mars explorers, aside from sampling the immediate surface they touch down upon, will be gathering information to help answer these questions and many more. No "lander" has yet reached the Martian surface and scientists do not know quite what to expect. Much more studying must be done before anyone can plan appropriately for an actual manned Mars landing. Space engineers do know that the first manned team will have to experiment on Mars just as early Apollo crews explored and experimented on the surface of the Moon. Basically, the Mars team will be using the same techniques and searching for the answers to many of the same questions. For this reason, they will be using either the same tools or modified versions of them.

The first manned Mars landing will be an epochal event in man's history, as well as one of the most anticipated achievements of the 20th century. When and if the landing occurs, and subsequently the return to Earth, then man will truly have been "out in space" and away from the gravitational pull and protection of his own planet. This achievement alone will be a great step forward for scientific technology, because if it is successful it will have established beyond any possible doubt man's capability of reaching still other planets in our Solar System.

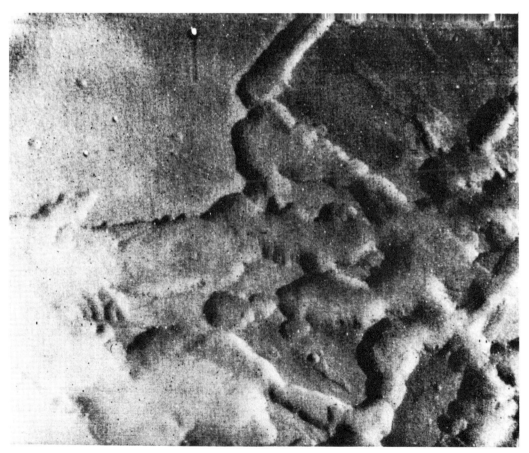

The "Grand Canyon" area of Mars, photographed by Mariner 9 in January, 1972, from 5,050 miles away, indicates that erosion possibly took place here. The canyons, about 6 to 12 miles wide, have smooth floors and are separated by flat surface mesas or plateaus.

Building a Home on Mars

To establish a permanent or semi-permanent base on Mars, space planners envision the use of three distinct pieces of equipment: a modified Apollo Mars Landing Module, one of the Baseline Space Station Common Modules, and a Rover type of vehicle. In concept, the Common Station Module will fit on top of the Landing Module (Mars Excursion Module) to create a sizable "house" in which the explorers can work, sleep and take refuge. The Rover will transport them over the Martian terrain.

The modified Mars Excursion Module will be considerably larger than the Command Module that carried astronauts to lunar orbit in the late 1960's and early 1970's. Movable couches used during the flight from Earth can be cleared away to provide room for the team to walk about inside the Module. Originally, there must also be space inside the Module to store the Rover; it can be "parked" outside the little base station once the team has landed. But it is the Baseline Common Module that will allow the team to do the necessary work of testing and experimenting.

Getting this hardware to Mars will be no easy task. Two simultaneous flights will have to be undertaken—one carrying the astronauts, another carrying the Common Module. The two separate parts can be joined together before the long voyage to Mars begins, or else they can be assembled after they both reach Mars orbit. NASA is still undecided which course to take, although assembly in Mars orbit seems the most likely.

A let-down ramp built into the Excursion Module will allow the Rover to be driven directly from inside the lander onto the Martian surface. The vehicle will be the team's sole method of covering great distances over the landscape. It will have to be changed in design from the original concept used on the Apollo 15 and 16 flights. On the Moon there was no noticeable atmosphere; no wind, no debris being blown through the air, no vapor in the air. It will be different on Mars, and perhaps total enclosure of the vehicle will be the best course. Present thinking suggests a fully pressurized vehicle for the sake of safety while on the Martian surface.

The first stages of a full Mars Base will certainly take other factors into account. The airlock again will be an important device to separate the station's Earth-atmosphere from the harsh Mars environment. With the Martian surroundings comes the problem of air in motion, with a water-content that may well cause corrosion and seepage. The Mars Base station will have to be doubly air-tight with back-up safety precautions. The explorers will continually have to guard against cross-contamination of Mars surface and station interior.

Where possible, the soil and surface materials of Mars can be used to help provide a packing round the station, perhaps even to construct a windbreak along some predetermined perimeter. In another instance, assuming the

MARS BASE

The bare minimum for a Mars Base would include use of a Baseline Space Station Module atop a Mars Excursion Module base support. This cutaway view shows plans for living quarters, medical facilities, a laboratory and a central control unit to monitor operations at remote sites on Mars.

surface material is as workable as the Moon's soil, it can be piled up over such objects as storage huts, radio gear and supplies. Future Mars Bases may well be built into the sides of craters or underground, where surface material is used as a protective covering. First, however, we must determine if the Mars soil contains any harmful radiation or bacteria, or other contents that would be detrimental to the astronauts or their instruments.

Assuming that the Mars descent stage and the Baseline Station Common Module arrived at the planet in two separate pieces, it would provide for two orbiting spacecraft—the "mother craft" for the manned descent stage (Excursion Module) and the booster for the Station Module. Conceivably, these two orbiting pieces of gear might be docked together to provide an orbiting Mars Space Station that can be manned or used for an orbiting storage container. When it is time for the astronauts to return to Earth, they can put the Station Module into orbit and transfer to the "mother craft" for the long trip home. This concept would also allow several crew members to remain in orbit for monitoring purposes while the astronaut/explorers remain on the surface of the planet. With astronauts in two separate places, a number of specialized experiments could be conducted between Mars orbit and Mars surface.

By the time we send a team to Mars for long-term exploration, the Space Shuttle will have had to become the workhorse of space. If it lives up to expectations, it will easily sustain the explorers on the surface indefinitely,

For a temporary Mars Base, several Mars Excursion Modules, a mobile laboratory (pressurized) and a drilling rig are planned.

adding to or subtracting from the main Mars Base. It will bring supplies, equipment and additional astronauts to the planet. In time, since Mars contains an atmosphere, landing strips can be cleared for the Shuttle to land near the Base station. As a base for taking on samples and spent supplies and for astronauts rotating duty, the station will endure as long as necessary; more importantly, it can be expanded to any size desired. If fuel is ferried to the Base station, this can turn the little three-man module station into a gigantic complex of buildings.

Scientists plan to use the same procedures for studying Mars that they used in finally landing on the lunar surface. The same carefully planned, almost strategical campaign will be adopted for all the planets. The Mariner spacecraft will first pass close by for testing the planet's atmosphere and gross surface characteristics, including some photography. Next, another orbiter craft will begin to map the planet and a search will be made for a potentially safe and scientifically desirable landing site. Then, astronauts will be sent to orbit the planet and study its characteristics from a safe distance—which also tests the capability of the spacecraft they are using. Finally, a small team will be sent to the planet to carry out short duration investigation. Eventually these "explorer trips" will become longer and longer.

This type of master plan for planetary study, proven successful in the march to the Moon, will be applied to each planet in turn. NASA has the ability to put the plan into effect immediately—the only drawback is money. NASA has to depend on Congress to appropriate the necessary funds. The Space Shuttle has been added to the budget and will do much to decrease costs by doing away with rocket launches and by providing a re-usable craft with a lifetime of 100 flights. The Mars plan will be used for Mercury, Venus, Jupiter, Saturn and Uranus, whenever explorations of those planets are approved.

Exploration and Survival

Scientists have performed admirably in overcoming the problems of space exploration, and they have gathered an absolutely immense storehouse of information in the process. They can prepare the astronauts for a manned Mars landing, keep them healthy and safe, and return them to Earth with a 95 per cent probability of success. But the first astronauts on Mars will have no past experience to draw upon. The remaining 5 per cent represents a high risk factor for the astronauts. It takes into account all the things not yet known about the planet, which may contain hidden dangers.

Armed with knowledge gained from Mariner flyby flights and photographic orbiters, and a Viking orbiting mission, scientists will have a good idea of what a Mars landing involves. That amount of knowledge will still represent only a tiny drop in the great ocean of unanswered questions, however.

By the time the explorers land on Mars, they will have had many practice trials and been able to modify their equipment extensively. On Mars, they will have to work far harder than their counterparts on the Moon ever did because of the one third gravity instead of the one sixth gravity of the lunar environment. Initial judgments will probably be faulty, especially in respect to distances because the explorer team will be on a far more alien terrain, one that is greatly influenced by an unfamiliar atmosphere. Mars' smaller size compared to Earth's will also affect the curvature of its horizon.

We studied the Moon for centuries through telescopes, and took pictures from the Earth that were enlarged to the greatest possible extent in order to examine fine detail. In addition, we had the experience of Ranger, Surveyor and Orbiter photos of the Moon to aid us. Scientists knew far more about the Moon before the first astronauts in Apollo 11 landed there than they will know about Mars. The primary concern, then, will be pure human survival. Astronauts have already demonstrated their physical ability to get to the Moon and back—but can they make it to Mars safely?

Scientists do not deal in speculation—they rely upon facts. Unfortunately, the facts where Mars is concerned are not yet clear. What will be discovered about the planet between 1972 and 1980 may very well revolutionize present concepts. Mariner 4, sending back pictures of craters on Mars, was one of the most astonishing surprises in the annals of scientific investigation. Scientists were totally unprepared for that jolting reality. The information sent back by the Viking project and additional Mariner photo-satellites may be just as amazing. The subject of Mars has still only barely been touched.

How, then, can astronauts safety be taken into account when no one yet knows what to guard against? That question cannot be fully answered until the first explorer pushes his booted foot across the Martian surface. On the other hand, one thing is already certain—that first astronaut will be thoroughly protected. He will have to stay close to the Mars lander module; he can traverse the landscape for only brief periods of time; he will have to be careful what he touches or steps upon; he will have to guard every step and every movement to protect his own life.

The Mars space suit will be an airtight container; the Mars Rover will be enclosed; the Mars Excursion Module will have to be airtight and provided with several whole back-up systems in the event of mechanical failure. Scientists are much more pessimistic about the Martian environment than the lunar environment, because they know far less.

Exploration will have the benefit of all those activities and instruments used to explore the Moon. In fact, the Moon by then may well have become an astronaut training ground where man, machines and instruments are tested for adaptation to planetary exploration.

For several years now, a number of special astronaut safety devices have been under scrutiny and development. Two are especially interesting and disclose the direction of present thinking: the immediate escape vehicle and the inflatable protection container. After considering what types of dangers there are to guard against, scientists have decided there are really only two protective actions that can be taken: sudden sheltering on the spot, as in the case of a meteorite bombardment, and leaving the scene altogether, quickly, in the face of certain disaster.

The inflatable protective container provides immediate shelter. A large rubberized tube, capable of being filled instantaneously with compressed air, would allow an astronaut to crawl inside it for protection. It can be carried in a small package and is inflated by means of a CO_2 gas bottle. It can ward off (literally bounce off) falling debris and can completely envelop a pair of men in seconds.

The immediate escape vehicle is a small encapsulated container that will hold two or three astronauts sitting inside it. Rigged with rockets and a parachute, it can be shot suddenly into the air for a long distance—and can be controlled by the astronauts for a short duration, down-range flight. A large drogue (anchoring) chute can be used to set the whole capsule down gently in another place. Other tools and research instruments will have to be

A semi-permanent Mars Base would need equipment of sophistication. More than just an expansion of the number of modules, the Base would require fuel and power plants, and a central shelter for housing operations-planning personnel, as shown here.

designed so that the astronauts' lives won't be placed in jeopardy when using these devices.

Unlike the lunar environment, which is virtually a vacuum, the Martian atmosphere is capable of transmitting sound. If the astronauts were able to walk about without a space suit, they would be able to hear noises and to talk with each other. Since the astronauts will be wearing space suits on Mars, however, scientists are confronted with a new aspect of space exploration. To take into account all the new possibilities inherent in the presence of sound, the planners must devise a method of mixing sound from the astronauts' voice communications system with sound occurring outside the astronauts' helmets. The problem is, how is it to be mixed so that the sounds don't become confused with each other?

Part of the answer lies in the fact that different sounds will *naturally* take care of themselves; radio transmissions will be heard as mechanical signals or spoken words, and any other sounds heard by the astronauts will immediately be recognized as originating on the Martian landscape. Still, there are two problems for which scientists have not yet found the answers.

One is the probability that some sounds on Mars will drown out voice communication between the explorers, and the other is that the astronauts might become accustomed to noises on Mars just as they get used to hearing noises on Earth. Perhaps the intent explorers will fail to recognize common or uncommon danger signals, such as the slowly building whistle of the wind at high speeds or the churning of Martian material being blown about or sliding as in a landslide. By the time the first astronauts journey to Mars, this dilemma will have to be resolved.

Bringing Mars Back Home

The science of geology makes use of basic principles developed during many centuries of trial and error. Many of these principles are physical laws, which geologists apply to this or that rock formation or geologic stratum. The Apollo astronauts found that the laws and principles of geology could be readily applied to rocks and other material found on the Moon. Sometimes new classifications had to be devised for newly discovered material. Future explorers on Mars will make use of these principles because they are laws of nature, not merely the laws of Earth geology. They *should be capable of application* on Mars, Jupiter or any of the planets and bodies in our Solar System.

The phrase "should be capable of application" is important, because if the first Mars astronauts find that known scientific laws do not apply to Mars, it would mean that that planet was created outside our Solar System. Such a finding would run counter to every known belief about the planets and especially about our Solar System. In general, then, scientists now believe that Mars can be explored in the same way and with much the same instruments that the Earth and the Moon are studied. Present returns from Mariner indicate Mars is a faithful member of our Solar System.

The astronaut-explorers on Mars will want to bring back with them as much Martian material as they possibly can. While this activity seems to pose no real problems, scientists realize it will have to be done with considerable care. Because Mars probably contains living forms of some kind, scientists are apprehensive about what hidden dangers the material might contain. They don't want to contaminate the Earth with life-damaging Martian organisms, so the returned material will have to be examined in isolation just as the first lunar material was investigated in the specially-built Lunar Receiving Chamber.

Material that the astronauts bring back will be carried in tightly-sealed containers and vessels to prevent cross-contamination. The astronauts will be taught what to expect on Mars, and will be instructed to gather a number of different kinds of soil samples—rock formations, loose soil, oddly-colored material, material that seems to be different from anything usually found on Earth. All the samples will be photographed in color before they are picked up or even moved. Once a rock is moved, the astronauts will have to photograph the place where it originally rested and gather material which lay underneath the rock. This method was developed during lunar exploration with exciting results.

This model of a space escape vehicle for a three-man crew was devised for Mars. The vehicle has four retrorocket engines, each providing a thrust of 1,000 pounds. It uses nitrogen freon cold gas propellant for the attitude control thrusters. The rockets and thrusters are strapped to the vehicle and are jettisonable. During re-entry the vehicle would be aerodynamically stabilized.

For the first time, astronauts will have to learn how to deal with a foreign liquid. At present scientists still don't know exactly what quantities will be evident on Mars. A large pool or pond seems rather unlikely but not impossible, and they expect the liquid to be more in the form of moisture. The astronauts cannot allow this moisture to evaporate before it gets back to Earth. If pools, ponds or streams are discovered, they will have to be sampled in more than one place—near the edges and, where possible, near the deeper portion also.

The astronauts will also have to collect vapors, such as frost, fog and cloud haze. This will require specially-designed containers not only to capture the material and seal it for the return trip, but to enable Earth scientists to open it and test it when the team returns. Certain Earth materials, such as metals and fabrics, will be purposely exposed to the Martian atmosphere for the length of time the astronauts are on the planet. These materials will then be sealed and brought back for time studies to see what will happen to them over long periods of time. Scientists want to know what chemical reactions will occur in the Earth materials as a result of being exposed to the Martian influence.

The great amount of Martian exploration and sampling suggests a rather large storage area aboard the returning spacecraft. Even more important, this storage space will have to be carefully designed—specially constructed drawers, bins, and airtight sealing systems. The astronauts will also be required to take many photographs while they are on Mars, using different kinds of film. Present planning also takes into account the use of magnetic tape to record the results of instrumented testing.

People on Earth want to know *what Mars sounds like.* Tape recorders will be set up on the Martian surface to record any sounds that might occur. What an exciting possibility that is—bringing back the sound of a Martian wind or storm, or hearing the crunch of the astronauts' boots as they walk across the Mars landscape. It will be the first time that people on Earth will ever hear actual sounds from the surface of another planet.

For the return trip to Earth, the astronauts will have to change their space suits, because the garments they have worn on Mars may contain material of an unknown nature. The suits used during exploration will have to be placed in a sealed container to prevent contamination on Earth. In addition, everything collected and removed from Mars will have to be checked constantly and watched during the return trip to determine if any significant, visible changes are taking place.

Once the Martian materials, and even the whole spacecraft itself, return to Earth, they will have to be quarantined for a period of time until scientists determine if they contain anything harmful to Earth life forms. The Martian rocks and soil, and containers of Martian liquid and life forms, will be placed in a sealed testing chamber immediately, just as the first lunar samples were quickly isolated. It will be an exciting time for science!

Return to Amazonis

There are so many enticing geographical features on Mars, scientists will be hard pressed to settle upon an exact landing area for the projected first flight to the planet in the 1980's. Chances are that the first few flights will be along the Martian equator, where scientists can expect the best possible "weather" conditions. One of these areas will certainly be the region known as *Amazonis*, a broad, flat range of relatively level ground compared to the rest of Mars.

Like the first landing on the Moon, the first exploration of Mars will serve to tell scientists and astronauts alike if most of our educated guesses were correct or faulty. From that first flight, they will increase our knowledge of Mars at least one-hundred-fold—because in spite of the great amount of instrumented exploration, only a thinking, reacting astronaut can give us the information scientists need to have. The first Martian landing will determine all future directions on Mars, including the modification of instruments and methods then in use. Each successive trip to the planet will be scientifically more productive than the journey that precedes it.

With new equipment and precious knowledge from the first landing, the second team of astronauts will be scientists intent upon learning. The risk of a crisis will be less, and the astronauts will be freer to concentrate on the tasks dictated by science. For this reason, Amazonis is an ideal landing site because it is less rocky and mountainous than other regions. While most of the return mission will be concerned once again with gathering surface material, making subsoil tests and photographing the terrain, there will be more time for actual exploration.

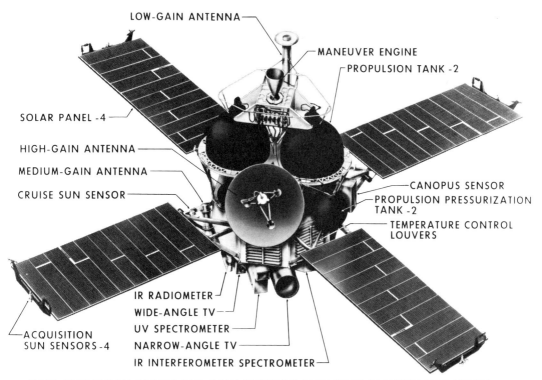

LOW-GAIN ANTENNA

MANEUVER ENGINE

PROPULSION TANK -2

SOLAR PANEL -4

HIGH-GAIN ANTENNA

MEDIUM-GAIN ANTENNA

CRUISE SUN SENSOR

CANOPUS SENSOR

PROPULSION PRESSURIZATION TANK -2

TEMPERATURE CONTROL LOUVERS

IR RADIOMETER

WIDE-ANGLE TV

UV SPECTROMETER

NARROW-ANGLE TV

IR INTERFEROMETER SPECTROMETER

ACQUISITION SUN SENSORS -4

NOTE: PROPULSION MODULE AND SCAN PLATFORM INSULATION BLANKETS NOT SHOWN

Mariner 9 with all its parts labelled.

The return to Mars, at Amazonis, will enable scientists to tap new sources of Martian terrain and environment and provide a second or third impression of what Mars is like. The stay-time will be extended so the astronauts can accomplish much more research. These men will no longer be simply spaceship pilots, but well-trained scientific investigators taught to conduct original types of technical research. They will be hard-working people from the planet Earth bent upon expanding the new science of planetary exploration—and developing the tools and methods necessary for a successful pursuit of knowledge. These astronauts will be far different from those who went before.

Amazonis is an amazingly expansive desert area. For science, its presence is a significant factor in the development of Mars' evolutionary process. Much of the Martian terrain is heavily cratered; a great deal of it consists of a tortured, twisted crust; the remainder is relatively flat and docile, like Amazonis. Scientists want to know why Amazonis has escaped the cataclysms that obviously have ruptured the rest of the planet. Since the Amazonian desert is near the Martian equator (0° to about 25° north), it is an ideal place to land.

Amazonis may not be devoid of craters—perhaps only fewer of them are to be found there. Mariner 4 showed a portion of the region marked by a number of shallow depressions. Mariners 6 and 7 missed the region altogether and concentrated their missions farther to the east. Mariner 9, an orbiter type of photographic craft, was successful in mapping a very large portion of Mars and passed over Amazonis. Pictures of the region have whetted scientists' appetites for a closer, longer look at the desert.

Near Amazonis are few of the rugged mountains, deep craters or canyon-lands common to other portions of Mars that help to break up sweeping winds which undoubtedly rage across the desert. Therefore, the astronauts will have to be on their guard. If the Moon was an absolute delight to scientists, Amazonis should prove to be a veritable feast of information.

Living on Mars

The first astronauts to set foot on Mars are expected to reach their destination sometime between 1980 and 1985, if NASA's plans are followed. Second and third teams will follow over the next several years until enough is known about the planet to enable a semi-permanent base to be established there. By then, several satellites will be in permanent Mars orbit—meteorological, photographic and communications craft to keep constant watch over the planet. The entire surface of Mars will have been precisely mapped, and highly accurate navigational and geographic charts will be available to the astronauts and the scientific community. Several Mars Space Stations will also be in polar and equatorial orbits.

If establishing a long-term Mars base with a projected active lifetime of about 10 years is possible, it will have to be undertaken in stages. Two teams of three astronauts each will be sent initially to prepare the selected area for receiving six to eight more teams. The landing area will have to be laid out; power sources and scientific instrumentation gear will have to be placed at specific sites; fuel containers and central communications systems will need to be strategically placed; preparation for the large base-type operation will be thorough indeed. When the planning is finalized, the word will go out to Earth from Mars: "Send the landing teams."

In pairs, the teams and their automatic cargo carriers will leave Earth to spend months on Mars. The cargo carriers, in the form of Space Shuttles, will continually ferry supplies and construction equipment to the designated area, and return for more supplies. As each Mars Excursion Module is landed, it will be permanently emplaced and will become one more Common Module in the Baseline Station system. And as each new team arrives, the scientists will take up their duties. The engineers especially will be busy.

To maintain and furnish power for as many as 8 to 12 Mars Base Modules will require considerable construction material in the form of pre-fabricated sections. The fuel depot will have to be designed for maximum safety; the central power source of nuclear generators will have to be set into motion; drilling operations will have to be begun to determine if underground

Anyone looking at this photo taken from a distance of 32,000 feet would be inclined to think it showed a barren, lifeless wasteland. It's not Mars, but Earth—the Grand Canyon in Arizona as photographed by the author. © by Thomas W. Becker.

minerals are available for common use. The communications systems (radio, television, laser) alone will require several weeks to set up and house. All the while, Shuttles will deliver supplies and equipment continually, and ferry men back and forth from the orbiting Space Stations to the Martian Surface Base for rotation duty.

Some scientists believe that, in time, it will be possible to change the oxygen content of Mars' atmosphere so that air for direct or re-cycled breathing can be generated right on the planet itself. Other planners want to construct a huge domed Mars Base so that astronauts and scientists can work and live in a "shirt-sleeve" environment. Still others feel it would be more logical and economical to build an underground city. Any or all of these concepts can be carried out in time.

To make Mars a habitable place to live and work in is essential from the standpoint of establishing scientific and engineering capability. The Mars Base is a means to an end—a method of surviving on Mars for an extended period of time in order to conduct research, and a means of establishing a foothold in the Solar System from which to reach still farther out into space. Like the Moon, Mars too will be a training ground for Jupiter and Saturn, until one day—in the far distant future—the astronauts will have attained a capability of breaking free of the Solar System.

Scientists know that there are changes on the surface of Mars that roughly correspond with changes of seasons on the Earth. This is not to say, however, that Mars has seasons—Autumn, Winter, Spring, Summer or anything else. By the time the Mars Base is established, however, they will know what to expect from Mars' weather and climate. Living on Mars will demand a number of changes in the astronauts' way of thinking. While Mars is similar to Earth in a few respects, it is different in a great many more.

To travel away from the Base, the Mars Rover vehicle that is being planned is very much like a mobile home. It is fully pressurized, contains all the necessary life support systems, and can virtually be lived in for many days up to a few weeks. The vehicle is far different from the Lunar Rover type of "dune buggy" used by the Apollo astronauts. It is a mobile chamber complete with airlock and windows, and it can be parked for overnight sleeping. Such a machine will enable the astronauts to roam over the Martian surface for 300 or 400 miles before having to return to the Base. During that time, they can leave the vehicle to take pictures or collect samples, and even conduct highly technical scientific experiments.

(Left) A planetary space vehicle powered by outboard nuclear rockets, such as might be used for a manned expedition to Mars. The central section consists of crew quarters and laboratories, a planetary landing module, and a third propulsion system for the return journey. (Right) A modular space station that could be assembled while in Mars or Jupiter orbit. The solar cell panels would provide electricity.

Phobos, Mars' innermost moon, was caught by the Mariner 9 computer also. It appears to be very old, with considerable structural strength. Its irregular shape may have been caused by asteroids hitting it. Large and small craters abound. This is a computer print-out enhanced by techniques conducted in the Image Processing Laboratory at JPL, Pasadena, California.

In time, other Mars Bases will have to be established, providing links across the Martian surface which astronauts and scientists can use. Crews will be continually rotated. Between surface bases on Mars and on the Moon, and orbiting stations in space, astronauts could conceivably stay in space for a year at a time, moving from one base or station to the other. Scientists do not yet know, though, how weightlessness will affect astronauts on such long stay-times, or what physical problems will arise from a constant environment of reduced gravity. On the other hand, it may be necessary to set up artificial gravity-type Space Stations to reduce physical complications.

Scientists will have to be content with studying Mars for its own rewards because the atmosphere will not permit improved astronomical observation. But there are enough unanswered questions where Mars is concerned, so that many decades will pass before astronauts unravel a mere several of its mysteries. Whatever the outcome, a permanent base on Mars will have resulted from tremendous technological advances. By the time such a base becomes a reality, Mars itself may well be a stopping place for men and machines moving to and from the other planets. Scientists will have created a new kind of life with its own peculiar advantages, to which thinking man will have to be quick to adapt. Astronauts of the future will find their "world" spread out before them among the planets of our Solar System, and they will be dreaming of some day reaching the stars.

3. EXPLORING THE SOLAR SYSTEM

Astronomers have arbitrarily separated our Solar System into two distinct parts: the Inner Planets (Mercury, Venus, Earth, Mars) and the Outer Planets (Jupiter, Saturn, Uranus, Neptune, Pluto). The Inner Planets have also been referred to as the Terrestrial Planets because they have some characteristics in common with our Earth, such as size and density. The Outer Planets are generally much larger and colder, and less likely to sustain life. Tiny Pluto is an exception, as it is located so far from the Sun, on the very fringe of our Solar System, that it must be very much like a ball of ice.

The Sun, the Asteroid Belt between Mars and Jupiter, and the interplanetary and solar winds and gases are also included as part of our Solar System. Other additions include comets, meteor shower groups, micro-meteorites, and the various magnetic fields and pressure systems occasionally encountered by satellites. Astronomers have contributed materially to efforts in space; in fact, without help from astronomers, the space scientists would have had a more difficult time knowing what to expect in space. Conversely, the explorations in space have completely revolutionized the science of astronomy. Many useful discoveries for astronomers have been made by satellites, photographic spacecraft and manned exploration missions.

Space scientists have adopted a logical, step-by-step schedule to explore our Solar System. Scientists in the program known as the "Balanced Strategy of Planetary Exploration" are already at work on such projects as the investigation of Mars, deep space probes, satellite sensing of the planet Venus, and various Earth-orbiting observatories to investigate the Sun. Until the 1960's, astronomers were confined to studying the heavens through telescopes, but space science investigations have carried highly technical instruments aloft to take pictures of planets and to conduct a wide variety of precise experiments out in open space.

No one can afford, however, simply to launch a lot of satellites in the hope they will send back some glimmer of information. NASA's efforts are planned and designed to return specific kinds of data about definite preselected objects and phenomena. The spacecraft must be precisely aimed at designated targets and programmed to send back the required information in a form that can be quickly understood and immediately applied. The instruments carried by these spacecraft have to be created to work infallibly

THE MILKY WAY GALAXY

ORBITS OF THE PLANETS

THE EARTH AND MOON

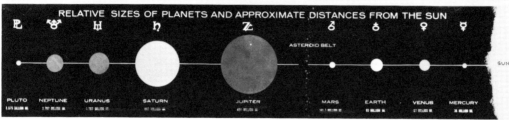
RELATIVE SIZES OF PLANETS AND APPROXIMATE DISTANCES FROM THE SUN

ASTEROID BELT

SUN

PLUTO | NEPTUNE | URANUS | SATURN | JUPITER | MARS | EARTH | VENUS | MERCURY

so as to measure what they are supposed to measure and to photograph exactly what has to be photographed.

All this activity leaves little or no room for error, because space research is costly and time-consuming. The spacecraft has to be launched towards a planet, for example, on an exact time schedule. If the spacecraft or its instruments are faulty, scientists may have to wait years for a similar opportunity.

The "Balanced Strategy of Planetary Exploration" is composed of missions of increasing difficulty and distance:

"Flyby" missions in which spacecraft pass close to a planet and scan it with instruments, as was done with Venus and Mars.

Atmospheric probe missions, in which spacecraft penetrate a planet's atmosphere but are destroyed in the process.

Orbiter missions, where spacecraft survey a planet from orbit, taking pictures and "reading" or "sensing" its physical and chemical make-up.

Lander missions in which the spacecraft soft-lands on the planet's surfaces, radios back certain data to Earth, and takes close-up pictures.

Sample-returning by means of manned first-missions which bring back samples of a planet's atmosphere and soil.

Extensive *manned exploration* of a planet by astronaut teams and by Rover vehicles.

Of these types of missions, only the first four are planned for the 1970's; manned planetary missions are expected to be attempted beginning in the 1980's, especially to Mars. Manned visits to other planets could begin in the 1990's and be carried into the 21st century by astronauts flying to the Outer Planets. The planet Pluto, however, will always be a problem to reach. Scientists will also sample and investigate the Asteroid Belt, any comets in the vicinity of the exploring spacecraft, and perhaps follow some of the meteor showers.

Since scientists have only just begun to explore space, they do not know what to expect in our Solar System. There is no physical, natural law that

MARINER MARS '71
MARS ORBITER 1971/1972

VIKING
MARS ORBITERS & LANDERS
1973/1974

PIONEER F & G
JUPITER FLYBY 1972/1973

HELIOS
INTERPLANETARY 1974 & 1975

MARINER MERCURY '73
VENUS & MERCURY FLYBY
1973/1974

NASA's plans for the decade of the 1970's. Some of these need approval by Congress.

says our Solar System must contain only nine planets; perhaps some day astronomers will discover others. Many other properties of the Solar System are undiscovered as yet, and the questions to be answered are truly awesome ones. In the process of exploring the planets, scientists will begin to uncover the meaning and composition of our Solar System, and begin to achieve such knotty objectives as:

To reconstruct accurately the origin and evolution of the nine planets, asteroids and comets, and the "interplanetary medium."

To recount accurately the origin and evolution of life within the Solar System.

To apply new-found knowledge of the other planets to the Earth so that we can understand the Earth better.

To determine what natural laws govern all the planets, individually and collectively, and if our Solar System is young or old.

To discover if there is a life form common to all the planets, or if the Earth is entirely alone with a unique life form system.

Scientists have already sampled Venus and Mars to a limited extent by use of the Mariner standard spacecraft. For the gigantic task of exploring the other planets, however, they will have to build spacecraft far more reliable than the ones already being used. A typical flyby mission to catch several planets at one time may require as many as eight or nine years—a long time for a spacecraft to continue to function in the extremes of interplanetary temperature and magnetic fields, and over such immense distances.

Mariner to Venus/Mercury

Since 1961, Venus has been the subject of intensive investigation almost equal to the many explorations of Mars. For Earthbound scientists, Venus is a tantalizing planet that always keeps itself veiled from view by a thick, never-ending blanket of atmosphere and clouds. Man's first physical contact with the planet came in 1961 when radar impulses were bounced back to Earth with the results only mildly satisfying. Scientists can partially diagnose Venus from these radar waves, as well as from the radio waves emitted by the planet itself.

Beneath its protective cloud cover, Venus is about the size of the Earth, but astronomers have no knowledge whatever of its topography. The planet rotates on its axis only about once in every 240 or 250 days. One of the most amazing facts about it, though, is that it *rotates backwards*, that is, east to west, a phenomenon scientists call "retrograde rotation." From the radar impulses scientists were also able to distinguish numerous "rough spots" on Venus' surface, but no one knows what these spots are.

The temperature of Venus is also a matter of some controversy. At first, scientists believed the temperature to be about –28° F (–33° C) until an error was found in the interpretation of the spectrographic analysis. Then, in 1956, astronomers announced they believed Venus' surface temperature registered a sizzling 800° F (426° C), and suddenly the possibility of life on our near neighbor completely vanished. The only way to really settle the question of temperature, as well as many other mysteries, was to sample Venus directly. That sampling began in 1962 with the spacecraft Mariner 2, a flyby planetary probe.

During a flyby, the spacecraft spends only a few hours in the vicinity of a planet. In that time, its instruments must accurately record as much as possible of the physical and chemical properties of the planet. Mariner 2 took 109 days to reach Venus—covering a distance of about 36,000,000 miles—and passed within 21,598 miles of the planet. The 447-pound craft made some profound discoveries.

The magnetic field round Venus was found to be close to zero; Venus seemed to have no radiation or solar plasma concentrations; it is not surrounded by a micro-meteorite or dust cloud like the Earth; its surface temperature is about 800° F (426° C), both by day and by night; there is only a small amount of carbon dioxide above the Venusian atmosphere. Scientists therefore supported the view of Venus as a "hot planet" and pretty well gave up all hope of finding it capable of supporting life.

On October 19, 1967, Mariner 5 passed within 6,300 miles of Venus and made some more discoveries. The craft's instruments confirmed the 800° F (426° C) temperature; a thick carbon dioxide atmosphere was found to exist; the planet has a very weak magnetic field, about 1,000 times less than Earth's; and most amazing of all, the Venus atmosphere traps electromagnetic waves entering it from outside and does not allow them to leave again. Very little is yet understood about this strange phenomenon. Scientists suggest that, to a person standing on Venus, the planet's horizon would appear to curve upward instead of downward as on Earth.

From what they have learned about Venus, scientists agree that they cannot be certain just what material the planet contains. The Mariner flights have served to spread considerable confusion about Venus; more flights will be needed to go back and try again, with better instruments and, hopefully, a closer look. The program to investigate Venus, as well as the planet Mercury, is called Mariner-Venus-Mercury, and was once scheduled to be launched in the Autumn of 1973, but probably will be delayed, due to lack of funds.

The Mariner spacecraft, when it is launched, will carry instruments that have been proven on other flights to photograph both planets and to measure the particles and fields surrounding them. The craft's instruments will also study their atmospheres and ionospheres. Mariner will make use of a gravity-assisted swing-by to within 3,300 miles of Venus (in February, 1974?), and to within 625 miles of Mercury (in the following March?). The spacecraft weighs about 900 pounds and is similar to the Mariners that have preceded it.

Mariner will be able to take about 5,700 picture frames of Venus and some 2,740 frames of Mercury. The pictures are expected to be every bit as good as those taken of the Moon by Ranger, Surveyor and Orbiter because of the improved 1500 mm Cassegrain telescopes placed on the two television cameras. And because three new 210-foot diameter antennae will be in operation by 1974, the television pictures can be received direct from the spacecraft instead of having to be coded and sent back as "bits" as was done by all the previous photo-spacecraft.

What are scientists looking for? They answer, "Anything, everything, whatever we can find—our knowledge about both planets is so meagre that anything at this point can be considered a major discovery." Mercury is so close to the Sun that astronomers have never been able to get a good view of it. Now, scientists will be able to map and identify some of its major physical landmarks, investigate its craters, determine the orientation of the spin axis, and search for its satellites. For Venus, scientists want to go back to confirm or deny previous suspicions about its cloud blanket, and to learn something

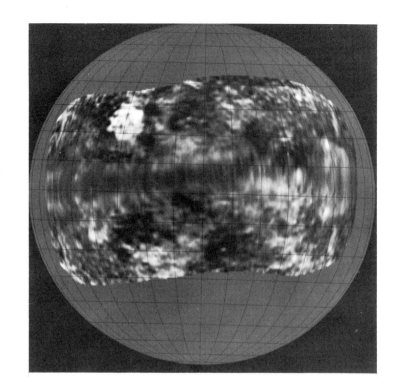

The largest map yet plotted of Venus was made by using radar beams. It covers 30 million square miles, or one sixth, of the planet's surface. The map-plot suggests mountain ranges, especially the bright spot at upper left.

about a mysterious ultraviolet "cloud" that appears to circulate round the planet every five days. Also, there are many long-term questions to be answered about each planet: what does its surface look like, how was it formed and when, exactly what kind of atmosphere does each planet have? The table on the next page shows the type of experiments that will be carried aboard Mariner-Venus-Mercury.

The Mariner craft will reach Venus first. Using its gravitational field as a propulsion instrument, the craft will be slowed down temporarily and then, as the gravity becomes less and less, the craft will be whipped outward like a ball on a string to streak toward Mercury. To accomplish this complicated manoeuvre, the first time it has ever been tried, Mariner will have to be aimed precisely toward a point out and away from Venus; the exact path Mariner takes will have to be calculated with the precision of a finely-tuned watch.

Venus must be much like an open furnace. The thick cloud covering extends up to about 35 miles from the surface, rather an incredible height when we think that the highest clouds on Earth never get higher than 10 miles. Such a thick cover must block out most of the Sun's rays; Venus is probably mostly dark, or at best only a soupy twilight. The surface features, bombarded by trapped solar energy that probably cannot break back out through the cloud cover, are likely to be boiled to a molten, seething mass in constant motion. This phenomenon is called a "greenhouse effect" by scientists.

Mercury's orbital path keeps it close to 43,000,000 miles from the Sun. Without a protective atmosphere, Mercury has a temperature ranging from about 650° F (343° C) in the daytime to about –300° F (–184° C) at night. This heated planet is undoubtedly cracked and scorched, containing a vari-split surface crust in the face of this constantly changing temperature harassment. Bombed continuously by meteors that are not burned up in a normal atmosphere, Mercury's surface is pock-marked by craters and fissures. In effect, Mercury probably looks much like our Moon. Its "year" is only

Scientific Instrumentation

Mariner to Venus/Mercury

INSTRUMENT	PURPOSE
2 television cameras with 1500 mm telescopes:	Study Venus' dense cloud blanket, and circling ultraviolet clouds. Map and identify Mercury's landmarks; determine spin axis orientation. Search for satellites of both planets.
Spacecraft transmitter and terrestrial receivers:	Provide radio communication on interplanetary phenomena during flight and at planetary encounters; information on atmospheres, ionospheres, radii, and surface characteristics.
Scanning Electron Analyzer:	Determine how solar wind interacts with Venus and Mercury, characteristics of solar wind between Earth and Mercury. Compare this data with similar data from Pioneers F and G between Earth and Jupiter.
Two triaxial fluxgate magnetometers:	Measure interplanetary magnetic field, and fields near Venus and Mercury. Study interaction of the solar wind with these planets.
Two ultraviolet grating spectrometers:	Search for Mercury's atmosphere and determine its structure and composition. Investigate the same at Venus.
Infrared radiometer:	At Venus, measure cloud-top and limb-darkening temperatures and search for holes in the cloud cover. At Mercury, measure surface-brightness temperatures and correlate infrared features with visible features.
Charged particle detector:	Study the charged particle bombardment of Mercury and the properties of charged particles reaching Mercury from solar flares.

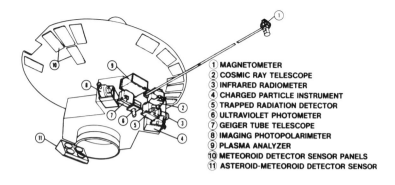

The separate mechanisms of Pioneer F, the small unmanned craft that will take the first close-up look at Jupiter and return data on about 20 aspects of the big planet and its moons and environment. It left Earth in early 1972.

1 MAGNETOMETER
2 COSMIC RAY TELESCOPE
3 INFRARED RADIOMETER
4 CHARGED PARTICLE INSTRUMENT
5 TRAPPED RADIATION DETECTOR
6 ULTRAVIOLET PHOTOMETER
7 GEIGER TUBE TELESCOPE
8 IMAGING PHOTOPOLARIMETER
9 PLASMA ANALYZER
10 METEOROID DETECTOR SENSOR PANELS
11 ASTEROID-METEOROID DETECTOR SENSOR

88 Earth days—but during the time that it revolves about the Sun, it turns on its axis one and a half times. Its "day" is then about twice as long as its year, or 176 Earth days.

Such are the strange habits of Venus and Mercury, and space scientists and astronomers are eager to know more about these bizarre happenings. By doing so, they hope to understand the Earth better, finding phenomena among the planets that are also common to the Earth—as well as some that are different. Scientists' interest is not confined merely to the other bodies and activities in our Solar System, but also to learn how the asteroids and other natural phenomena relate to the Earth and to our Moon.

Pioneer to Jupiter

Moving outward from the Sun, Mars is the last of the Inner Planets. Just outside the orbit of Mars is the area of the Asteroids, a curtain of debris and material ranging in size from dust particles to chunks of solid material nearly 500 miles in diameter. The next planet is Jupiter, the first of the Outer Planets and the largest in our Solar System. The mystery of Jupiter and its features has fascinated scientists for centuries; soon, possibly in 1973, scientists will begin to learn something about it at last.

Like all the planets, Jupiter has a personality and a character of its own. It spins about completely once every 9 hours and 55 minutes, and bulges at its equator because of its rapid rate of rotation, while its surface features change shape and color like a space-age chameleon. The color-shifting atmospheric bands, made up of layers of frozen and liquid ammonia, cascade wildly across an interior characterized by heavy pressure and crackling storms. Underneath this strange, heavy atmosphere, the planet's surface may be composed of pressurized hydrogen.

One of the greatest mysteries is the nature of the Great Red Spot that appears like a gigantic gouged-out wound slowly marching across the lower part of this twirling planet. Just as intriguing to astronomers and space scientists is the fact that Jupiter may be most like the primitive environment

PIONEER FLIGHT TOWARD JUPITER

MAGNETIC FIELD
RADIATION BELTS
VISUAL IMAGING

JUPITER

ASTEROID BELT

SPACECRAFT

from which life actually sprang—an atmosphere of hydrogen, methane, water and ammonia that scientists believe describes the Earth as it was some $4\frac{1}{2}$ billion years ago. Eleven times the diameter of Earth, Jupiter has also been described by scientists as the Solar System's "second star" because it gives off more energy than it receives. Temperatures, scientists theorize, must range from about $-200°$ F ($-128°$ C) at the tops of the cloud cover to about $20,000°$ F ($11,093°$ C) at the planet's core.

Jupiter sends out random, strong gushes of radio energy and, aside from the Sun, is the strongest source of radio signal broadcasting in our heavens. These broadcasts seem to be tied to some of Jupiter's moons, especially Io. The planet has its own family of 12 natural satellites to keep it company; one of the moons, Ganymede, is larger than the planet Mercury. This large moon is also a primary target for scientists.

There is a great deal we want to know about Jupiter, as this lists suggests:

☐ Does Jupiter have a solid surface? (Only its cloud cover can be seen in our telescopes.)

☐ What is the chemical composition of Jupiter and its strange cloud layers?

☐ Is there life on Jupiter? What is it like, and how much is it like life on Earth?

☐ Why does Jupiter change color, and are these changes linked with the 11-year solar cycle, as some scientists believe?

☐ What is the nature and strength of Jupiter's radiation belt?

☐ Are Jupiter's radio emissions linked in any way with its larger satellites, as seems to be the case?

☐ Are some of the moons of Jupiter really smaller planets trapped in a Jovian orbit? How much are they like or unlike Earth?

☐ Since the Earth and Jupiter are so different, do the magnetic fields of each have different origins?

☐ Where does Jupiter's energy come from?

☐ What is the nature of the Great Red Spot?

An artist's rendering of a Pioneer-type spacecraft passing close to the mammoth planet Jupiter, which is 1,000 times the size of the Earth, but spins more than twice as fast.

For a long journey through the cold void of space, heaters are needed to protect vital equipment on the spacecraft. On this Pioneer craft are two sets of radio-isotope thermo-electric generators (RTG's) developed by the Atomic Energy Commission for this purpose and to power the craft. The Pioneer is the first spacecraft to depend on RTG's as a primary source of power. Arrows point to one set of them in this artist's rendering.

As soon as one question seems answered, a dozen more are raised in its place. All are intriguing, all relate not only to the Solar System, but to Earth as well. Each question is extremely important.

The first Pioneer to Jupiter was rocketed up in early 1972. Its journey to Jupiter will be a long one, approximately 500 million miles. It will take the spacecraft nearly two years to reach there. Such a long time and distance worked heavily against space scientists who had to design a craft small enough and of such little weight that a minimum amount of on-board fuel is required during the flight. To solve the problem, scientists at the Ames Research Center, at Mountain View, California, hit upon an already-existing type of spacecraft as the ideal instrument carrier—the Pioneer. Their work on a modified Pioneer, begun in 1969, gained from experience

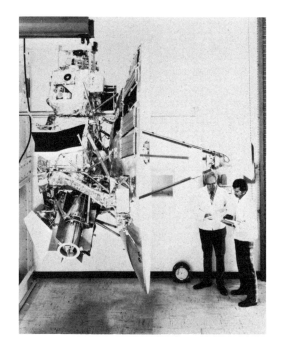

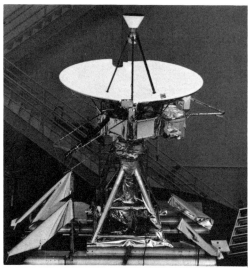

The small size of the Pioneer F spacecraft is evident in this photo. The picture also offers a good look at one of the RTG devices. (Above) The Pioneer spacecraft is ready for shipment to the launch pad.

with four previous Pioneer flights into deep space. The new craft, called Pioneer F (or 10 upon launching), bears little resemblance to previous configurations.

Another set of problems has had to be taken into account where Pioneer F is concerned; the craft also must carry out three separate duties:

1. Study the interplanetary material between Earth and Jupiter.
2. Determine the nature of the Asteroid Belt.
3. Develop the required technology for future flights to the Outer Planets.

The basic design of the craft, then, had to include the capability of transmitting information across a vast distance of hazardous space while at the same time receiving far less solar power to activate and sustain its instruments as the craft gets farther and farther from the Sun. Pioneer F is an amazing machine indeed!

Instead of solar cell panels, Pioneer F has two pairs of radio-isotope thermo-electric generators (called RTG). Mounted on long booms (arms) away from the spacecraft, they can each generate an average of 120 watts. It will be the first time a spacecraft has ever used the RTG assembly. But the new electronic generators, if properly developed and able to withstand the long, agonizing voyage, will open up a new era in space exploration.

The little Pioneer has three hydrazine engines each with a thrust of about one pound that will accomplish mid-course corrections to keep the craft aimed at its far-distant target. Pioneer will be cooled by louvres to keep

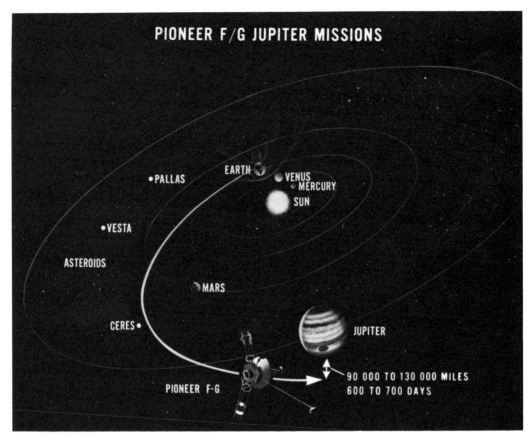

PIONEER F/G JUPITER MISSIONS

PALLAS
EARTH
VENUS
MERCURY
SUN
VESTA
ASTEROIDS
MARS
CERES
JUPITER
PIONEER F-G
90 000 TO 130 000 MILES
600 TO 700 DAYS

This chart shows how Pioneer F will fly to investigate Mars and the Asteroid Belt, and come within about 100,000 miles of the surface of Jupiter on a journey that could take almost two years. After passing Jupiter, the craft will swing out into space and continue travelling until it disintegrates.

internal temperatures between –20° F (–28° C) and about 90° F (34° C). A 9-foot paraboloid S-band antenna will transmit 1,000 information bits per second from Jupiter across the distance to Earth. All the instruments on board are contained in boxed compartments.

Thirteen separate experiments have been selected for Pioneer F; half of these will be carried out before the spacecraft ever reaches Jupiter. If something goes wrong and the craft misses Jupiter by a wide margin, the mission can still be termed a success if the experiments conducted in transit to the planet are successful.

Let's imagine for a moment that we have hitched a ride on a Pioneer F, and that we can watch all that is happening aboard it and in deep space.

Pioneer is launched by an Atlas-Centaur rocket into an Earth-parking orbit. A few minutes later the Centaur upper stage will boost the spacecraft into an interplanetary transfer ellipse. Pioneer will suddenly be fired forward at a tremendous velocity, eventually reaching 32,400 miles per hour—the fastest speed ever attained by a space vehicle. Suddenly, Pioneer will be free of the booster as the metal plates (called a shroud) disconnect and fall away behind the shooting vehicle. The two booms containing the generators will arch out sideways, and the long arm containing the magnetometer will snap and lock into place. Pioneer is ready to begin its mission, streaking through space at roughly one fourth the speed of light.

The first event will occur as the craft enters the advanced area of the Asteroid Belt. By now, the sensing instruments are fully working and sending back a stream of information to Earth-based antennae expectantly turned skyward. The warmth of the Sun is just beginning to fade, because the craft has already passed Mars' orbital limit. Micro-meteorites continue to strike haphazardly against the metal of the craft's frame and instrument covers. None will be strong enough to penetrate, but occasionally the craft will have to right itself. Passing into the main stream of asteroids, Pioneer will now be 200 days from Earth and a full one third of the distance to Jupiter—about 140 million miles.

The Solar Wind will press against the metal structure where its presence

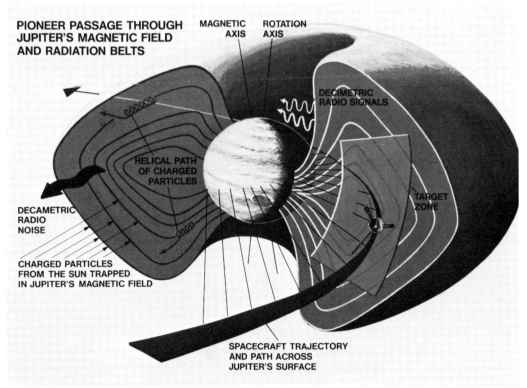

Diagram of Jupiter's magnetic field and radiation belts. The Pioneer F-G series of craft will offer the first close-up measurements of these Jovian phenomena.

will be recorded and, acting like a wounded bird, Pioneer will react by whining its indignation back homeward. The asteroids will become larger, some of them now the size of golf balls. As the craft plummets onward, the asteroids will grow bigger and bigger—there is a fear of impending collision because some of the asteroids are several miles in diameter. If one of them should hit Pioneer, the mission will be tragically ended. Quickly, the craft's detectors must sense out the nearby chunks and radio the discoveries to Earth: size, physical and chemical composition, speed of travel.

Here and there Pioneer will go through traces of ill-defined matter, plasmic material hoisted about by invisible magnetic fields. In the distance, the vehicle may cross the path of a comet. The presence of the fiery comet will be registered on instruments—its effect may loom threateningly, then will drop suddenly as Pioneer speeds doggedly on towards its target far in the distance. On Earth, scientists order Pioneer to change its direction slightly; the craft dutifully obeys by emitting short rocket bursts, and once again Pioneer is aimed like a well-shot arrow toward Jupiter.

Reaching two thirds of the distance into its mission, Pioneer will have lost all detection of the Sun's heat. Interplanetary matter will continue to brush against the craft and be carefully recorded. More than a year after the vehicle was shot upward from its pad at Cape Kennedy, all the systems continue to function without error or respite on the hardy little craft. It will now begin to pick up the first indications of an enormous mass in its path. The Geiger counter will sputter occasionally; galactic and solar protons and electrons will beat down on Pioneer's instruments. They will be faithfully noted.

As the lonely vehicle begins the last leg of its journey on its 680th day, it will pass within 100,000 miles of Jupiter. The view will be magnificent; the Pioneer instrumentation systems will pile up data so quickly the bits cannot be relayed to Earth fast enough. The craft's memory banks will begin to store the bits before releasing them. Jupiter will be scanned cleanly like a shower washing over a bather's body: magnetic field, magnetosphere, trapped radiation, charged particles, the heliosphere, ratios of hydrogen to helium and the refractory capability of the Jovian ionosphere and atmosphere, even Jupiter's satellites will be scanned by the searching of Pioneer's precision instruments.

It will all happen quickly. Very soon, in a matter of days, Jupiter will loom huge and awesome and then will begin to shrink as Pioneer is whipped like a stone in a slingshot on out past Jupiter into interstellar space to continue its journey. On and on it will travel, growing weaker.

In time, captured by the gravity of some unknown stellar wanderer, it will crash and be heard from no more. On Earth, its death will be lost in the excitement of newer space probes and greater discoveries. Such is the trip begun by the first Pioneer that left Earth in 1972 bound for a Jupiter flyby.

Touching the Outer Planets

Before Pioneer F completes half its voyage to Jupiter, a second Pioneer spacecraft is expected to be launched toward Jupiter with much the same mission but timed and aimed to pass the planet in another area. Scientists know that information from merely one particular region of Jupiter will give them only a sample and not enough facts about the whole planet to build a good body of knowledge. Such a short-sighted approach would be like a spacecraft sent from Jupiter to Earth that just happens to pass across the Pacific Ocean and from this deduces that the planet Earth is made up wholly of water.

Once every 175 years, the four Outer Planets are lined up in space in such a way that a single spacecraft has the rare opportunity of flying by all of them—Jupiter, Saturn, Uranus and Neptune. Such a scientific feast—with the opportunity of learning a great deal about three or four planets in one grand shot—could well change our entire concept of the Solar System and maybe even of the universe. Upon reflection, however, planners have come to believe that several shorter flights catching two or three planets at a time will prove more beneficial.

There are two such excellent opportunities: one in 1976–77 would include Jupiter, Saturn and Pluto in one long sweep, and another in 1979 would take in Jupiter, Uranus and Neptune. Both flights are now being considered, but again, time is not on the side of the scientists. An entirely new spacecraft will have to be built, tested and launched in a very short time because the Pioneer craft will probably not be suitable for such a long mission. Each of these flights would take more than eight years to complete and a far more reliable spacecraft than Pioneer is needed to last that long out in the cold expanse of space. What amazing flights they would be!

Astronomers have watched Saturn, the ringed giant, through telescopes for centuries, and seen its rings turn this way and that. Even the ancient Greeks and Romans were aware of the presence of Saturn. Without its rings or its 10 "moons," Saturn is still nine times the diameter of Earth. It turns on its axis once every 10 hours and 23 minutes, but takes almost $29\frac{1}{2}$ years to complete its voyage round the Sun. Now scientists would relish a chance to "touch" Saturn with the sophisticated instruments of a new kind of science, hoping to learn something of great value.

Scientists have long observed the appearance of different colored bands around Saturn. For many years, it was thought there were only three rings, until in 1969 a very faint fourth ring was discovered by French astronomer Pierre Guerin. Between two of the outer rings, there is a noticeable gap, known as the Cassini Division.

Scientists have offered two possible explanations for the presence of the rings: first, that they are planetary material that never congealed into a mass to form a planet, and, second, that they are the remains of a planet that passed too close to Saturn and broke up because of the giant's great gravitational pull. Some scientists believe the material actually consists of chunks of ice or ice-covered pieces of rock, each having its own orbit around Saturn, and numbering in the millions of separate pieces. A sensing spacecraft in a flyby of Saturn might very well settle these questions.

Saturn's composition is probably much like Jupiter's, with a heavy blanket of gases. Its mass is far less than Jupiter's, though, which may account for its equatorial bulge—the planet cannot seem to gather itself together into a compact ball. Still stranger is Saturn's low density, about seven tenths the density of water; the planet would therefore float upon the water if it could be put into a tub. And stranger still is Saturn's satellite Titan with a diameter of about 3,000 miles; it is the only moon in the Solar System that has an atmosphere. Some scientists have theorized it is really a trapped planet.

The planets Uranus and Neptune are so far distant from Earth that little is known about them other than what has been observed through telescopes. Facts about these other planets are aggravatingly elusive, and even their periods of rotation are still matters of speculation. Uranus is about 2,000,000,000 miles from the Sun, a cold green lifeless ball that takes 84 years to make one orbit. For half that time, its north pole is tilted toward the Sun; for the other half, the pole is tilted away and in total darkness. Uranus has five satellites and is nearly four times bigger than the Earth. Some scientists have reported vari-colored bands stretching round the planet.

Neptune, the outermost of the giant planets, is 3,000,000,000 miles from the Sun and can be little more than a ball of ice although scientists suspect it may have an atmosphere of ammonia ice and helium. Neptune's revolution round the Sun takes the equivalent of 164 Earth years. A day on Neptune is probably close to 15 hours, but again this fact has been difficult to determine. Neptune is about the same size as Uranus—almost four times larger than the Earth—and has two satellites.

Pluto, the most distant planet and the most recent to be discovered, is probably nothing but a frozen wasteland 40 times the Earth's distance from the Sun. It is so distant that the measurements already made of it are not trustworthy. Scientists do know that it makes one revolution of the Sun in 247 Earth years, and has a rotation of about $6\frac{1}{2}$ Earth days. Pluto has no observable satellites.

The distances between the Outer Planets are so vast that scientists really know little about any of them as compared to their knowledge of the Inner or Terrestrial Planets.

At one time, a mission known as Grand Tour was under consideration by the National Aeronautics and Space Administration; it was to include one

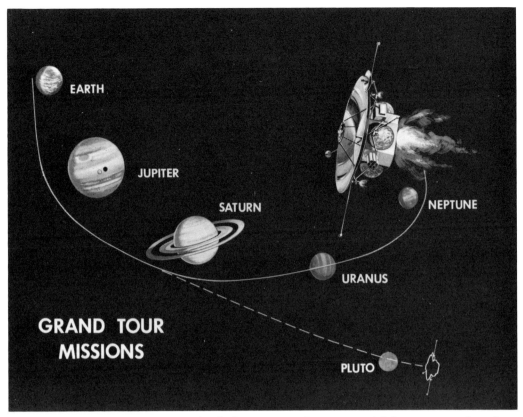

The unmanned "Grand Tour" of the outer planets could be an amazing feat of space exploration, if it is ever approved by Congress. The gravity of Jupiter would increase the spacecraft's velocity, and whip it towards Saturn. Saturn's gravity would whip it past Uranus, which in turn would whip it past Neptune. An alternative path would take it past Pluto from Saturn. The craft would have a propulsion system for changing its path.

or both of the flyby flights previously described. At the moment, however, it has been given secondary priority, and shorter Mariner flights to Venus and Mercury are being given preference to Jupiter and Saturn. This also makes more facilities and funds available for completion of the all-important Space Shuttle. This does not mean, however, that Grand Tour has been abandoned, only that it has been temporarily suspended. It could be taken up again in another form or even in its original concept provided there is enough time to prepare a new spacecraft design.

The shorter flights to the Outer Planets have been unofficially termed The Mini-Tours, and to carry them out successfully a craft called Thermo-electric Outer Planets Spacecraft (TOPS) is being designed by Pasadena's Jet Propulsion Laboratory scientists. The vehicle is a basic multi-purpose craft and combines long-life reliability with priority scientific instrumentation. TOPS has a stabilized scan platform, like the one used on the Mariner flights, that will permit the use of highly sensitive instruments to sense out and measure precise phenomena of the planets.

TOPS will also make use of new developments in high-frequency communications that speed up the process of relaying data back to Earth. Another recent break-through in spacecraft design involves a new concept of adaptive control with self-test and repair. The spacecraft will be able to switch itself to subsystems if primary functions go awry. Like the Pioneer F and G spacecraft, TOPS will be powered by radio-isotope thermo-electric generators, but of greater capacity.

Incredibly, the self-test and repair (STAR) computer can manage and control all spacecraft functions independent of any commands from Earth. Such a mechanism promises unprecedented advances in spacecraft reliability in the future. The STAR function uses highly miniaturized electronic microcircuits for an amazing compact and competent package weighing only about 30 pounds. It is guaranteed to operate for at least 10 years and, truly a child of the space age, it portends future spacecraft that can "think and act for themselves."

Sensing the Sun

For all people in all times, the Sun has been the custodian of life on Earth. In the strictest sense, it governs our total environment and is the focal point of our existence. It gives us warmth and light to see by, makes things grow and sometimes makes them die, sustains life-giving chemical reactions, and provides innumerable changes in all the phenomena known to our planet. Without the Sun, all life would cease. It is vitally important for the peculiarly fortunate inhabitants of Earth to learn as much about the Sun as possible.

Man has studied the Sun as long as he has studied any phenomenon on Earth, but only in recent years have scientists had the benefit of sophisticated tools to increase that study and the knowledge that comes from it. Scientists have managed to accumulate an impressive file on the Sun and its habits, yet there are plenty of gaps in our knowledge of the Sun. If scientists are ever to understand the Solar System, and eventually our galaxy, they will have to learn much more about the most awesome of our Solar System members— the raging, belching, magnificent inferno we call the Sun. As an object of study, the Sun is a typical specimen of the most numerous class of stars in the universe.

Since 1962, there have been six successful launches of Orbiting Solar Observatories. During the decade of the 1970's, four more OSO craft are planned to be put into Earth orbit; much of the work to be done by Skylab involves direct solar investigation; and a specially designed craft called Helios is expected to be launched first in 1974 and followed by a companion in 1975. All these Sun-studying craft will furnish scientists with a completely

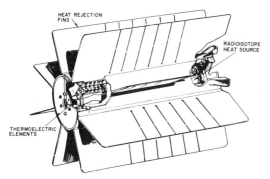

Diagram of SNAP-27 heat generator.

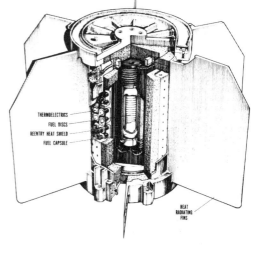

Diagram of SNAP-19 radio-isotope thermo-electric generator (RTG).

new concept of our star. In addition, some earlier solar and interplanetary probes returned considerable information about the Sun's activities.

A new and exciting spacecraft, and the first of its kind ever to be built, Helios is the result of an agreement between West Germany and the United States to launch two Sun-sensing spacecraft. The vehicle is being designed and built by a group of German scientists headed byMesserschmitt-Bolkow-Blohm GmbH with the assistance of America's General Electric Company. NASA has agreed to furnish the launch vehicle, launch pad and Cape Kennedy facilities, as well as the services of the Deep Space Tracking Network.

Helios' task will be to measure the structure and time variation of the plasma, cosmic rays and magnetic fields in interplanetary space as they are

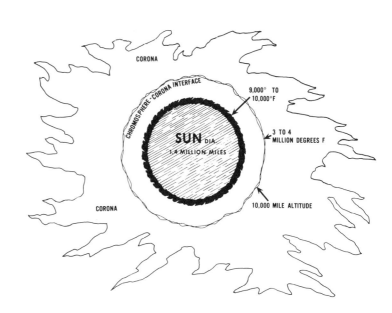

Helios and other orbiting Solar Observatories will begin to study the chromosphere-corona interface.

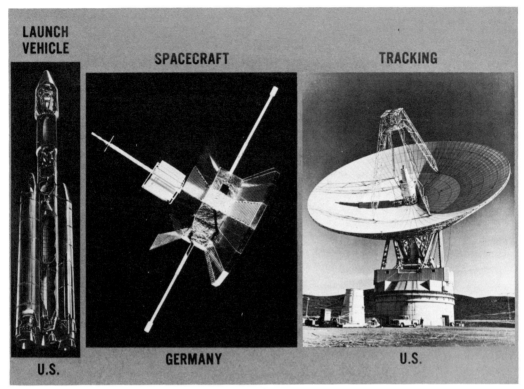

LAUNCH VEHICLE   SPACECRAFT   TRACKING

U.S.   GERMANY   U.S.

The Helios Solar Probe, planned for 1974 and 1975, was designed by West German scientists for launch and tracking by NASA facilities. It will venture three quarters of the distance to the Sun, and has to survive a heat intensity equal to 16 times that on Earth.

controlled by solar processes and events. It will be the first time that a solar probe came so close to the Sun—a distance of about 31 million miles. Helios' task will be difficult, and will require that the sturdy craft withstand great pressures and temperatures at a close distance from the Sun. Special heat-reflecting liquid coatings that can be painted on the spacecraft are being developed in hopes it will help reduce the intensity of the heat.

Essentially, Helios is a cylindrical configuration with a narrowed waist and ends that protrude outward. Four long booms jut out of the waist and another boom and an antenna protrude directly out of the top. The craft is spin-stabilized so that its spin axis is always perpendicular to the plane of the ecliptic. Over-all, it weighs about 425 pounds. This type of design did not occur by accident.

Because of the intense heat that is built up on a flat surface in the direct path of the Sun's rays, the Helios craft has slanted ends containing solar cells that have been pitched so that solar rays will strike them at an angle. The solar cells are interspersed with equal-sized, metal-backed mirror blocks that help disperse the heat rays and drain heat away from the solar cell patches. The flared ends of the spacecraft have the appearance of a checkerboard.

A second and much more difficult problem in Helios' design centers round the great distance to be covered in communication between the craft and the Earth's tracking and data-acquisition antennae. In order to reach Earth, Helios' telemetry transmitter power must be focused in a very narrow beam. To accomplish this, a parabolic reflector is mounted behind the antenna on top of the spacecraft. Unfortunately, though, because Helios is spin-stabilized, it rotates constantly so that at times the reflector is not pointed toward Earth. To overcome the problem, scientists designed the reflector to spin in the *opposite* direction from Helios' spin so that it remains pointed Earthward while the spacecraft turns beneath it. Space scientists call this a "mechanically despun" antenna—Helios is the first craft it has ever been tried on.

Ten different experiments are planned for each Helios mission. The two craft are expected to be launched approximately a year apart; the first is now scheduled for July, 1974, and the second for October, 1975. Luckily, solar probes do not have to wait for planets to move into the "right position" or to get themselves aligned. Some of the Helios duties are:

- ☐ Measurement of the solar wind velocity.
- ☐ Measurement of the interplanetary magnetic field close to the Sun.
- ☐ Measurement of low frequency fluctuations in the interplanetary field.
- ☐ Measurement of certain radio waves and plasma waves.
- ☐ Measurement of solar and galactic cosmic ray energies.
- ☐ Measurement of solar X-rays.
- ☐ Counting of solar electrons.
- ☐ Observation of zodiacal light wavelength and polarization.
- ☐ Measurement of the masses and energies of cosmic dust particles.

Helios will have a heliocentric Earth orbit so that at perihelion (point of closest approach) it will be only 31 million miles from the Sun, and at aphelion (most distant approach) about 93 million miles. The orbital period of 200 days will bring the craft closest to the Sun at specified intervals; that is, 100, 300, 500 days, etc., after launch. Because of its unique and sturdy design, Helios is expected to have a very long lifetime and to be capable of returning a steady stream of data constantly during that lifetime.

The Need to Know

Curiosity—a prodding urge to try new things and to experience new adventures—continually pushes some men toward newer and untried horizons. This is especially true in the exploration of space. What a scientist does not know about space has become every bit as important as the things he does know; that is why each new discovery prompts hundreds of questions.

Scientists, to satisfy their curiosity, invent and create and build new tools to find answers and to take them to outer space. The scientist thus becomes educated for a purpose; he learns equations, investigates objects, invents new computers and new methods, and solves complicated problems because they will serve to help him cross the frontiers of space.

There is also another kind of need to know that ranks in importance with human curiosity. The more scientists learn, *the more they must learn* in order to arrive at intelligent conclusions. They no sooner discovered from Ranger, Surveyor and Orbiter what the Moon was like than they immediately began to find a way to get closer. Finding this way posed innumerable new problems that had to be solved, and turned their attention to discovering or inventing machines and methods to put an astronaut on the lunar surface. After the first astronauts arrived at Tranquility Base in 1969, a whole new set of problems and questions arose about the lunar environment and about the astronauts' ability to survive and work there.

Perhaps some day an astronaut team will voyage beyond our Solar System, and eventually beyond our galaxy. As astronomer and science writer Arthur Clarke has often noted, "If man has thought about it, eventually it will be done."

All the little problems must be solved first; scientists must learn about the environments of the planets, and how an astronaut can reach those planets and live through the experience to bring back new knowledge. They have to know exactly what the properties of the Sun are, and what the Solar Wind is and does, before risking exposing human life to it. Learning about such things will lead scientists and engineers to invent new methods of measuring and surviving.

The vast expanse of deep space is so huge that science has had to create new yardsticks to measure it. Astronomers devised the *Astronomical Unit* as a measure of distance. It is the mean distance from the Earth to the Sun. Therefore, 1 A.U. equals about 93 million miles, and the Earth is 1 A.U. from the Sun. Jupiter is 5.20 A.U. away, Saturn 9.52 A.U. and little Pluto 39.37 A.U. from the Sun. But this yardstick proved to be still too small for certain distances.

The nearest star, not counting the Sun, is 25,000,000,000,000 miles away. Such a cumbersome number is far too difficult to name or work with, and is certainly beyond human comprehension. For convenience, scientists measure such a distance in terms of a *light year*, or the distance a beam of light will travel in a year at its speed of 186,282 miles per second. Proxima Centauri and Alpha Centauri, the nearest stars to us, then are only 4.3 light years away. When an astronomer looks at Proxima Centauri, he sees it as it looked 4.3 years ago, not as it is now. By this means of interstellar measurement, the star Sirius is 8.7 light years away. Some day, astronomers may learn that

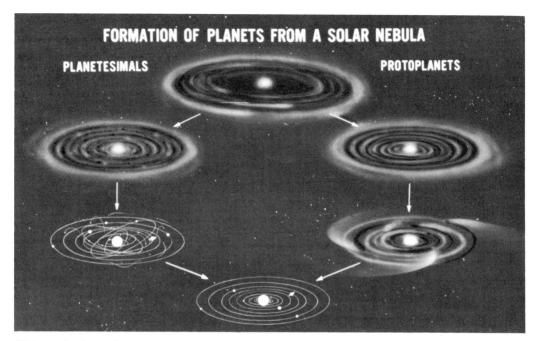

FORMATION OF PLANETS FROM A SOLAR NEBULA

PLANETESIMALS

PROTOPLANETS

This painting shows two possible theories about the formation of our Solar System from a Solar Nebula—either by a combination of stars in the nebula joined by gases and stellar debris, or by a massive star splitting up into orbiting satellites.

Sirius has a solar system of its own containing planets very similar to Earth. By the time they make such a discovery, several centuries from now, they will have mastered our Solar System and be using instruments and spaceships that are now wholly beyond human imagination.

For the next three decades, however, scientists will be exceedingly busy trying to settle one big question about our Solar System, namely, how it was formed. Centuries of astronomical observation have uncovered many natural laws at work in the Solar System, and scientists are finding that the cluster of planets and other phenomena whirling about the Sun represent a remarkably orderly environment. Where there is confusion in their knowledge or their impressions of the Solar System, it is apparently caused more by their own ignorance than any lack of cooperation on the part of nature.

Scientists hold three separate but logical theories about the creation of the Solar System:

1. "One Piece" Theory—the Sun, planets, asteroids, gases and other phenomena were once all one piece that broke up and spewed out all the objects which then began to revolve about the Sun.

2. "Trap" Theory—the contents of our Solar System were trapped into their present positions by the gravitational pull of the Sun as these objects passed through the galaxy.

117

3. "Explosion" Theory—the planets, their satellites, comets, etc., exist as the result of a collision of bodies or the explosion in space of one single body.

All three theories have their adherents and all have, at present, at least, enough evidence to support them. Only by concentrated study will anyone ever be able to determine for certain just how the Solar System came into being. This means placing a team of scientists on each planet in turn, finding phenomena common to all the planets, or discovering evidence to disprove any or all of the present theories, or adopting a completely new theory. The pursuit of this knowledge is one of the more exciting adventures in space science.

One of the leading students of the Sun and the Solar System is Dr. Gerard P. Kuiper, noted astronomer at the University of Arizona, who has quietly insisted, about the Solar System, "It is not a foregone conclusion . . . that the problem has a scientific solution. For instance, an enclosure in which the air has been stirred gives, after some delay, no clue on the nature or the time of the stirring. All memory of the event within the system has been lost." If Dr. Kuiper is correct, solving the dilemma over the birth of the Solar System will be highly difficult at best. We hope the "memory banks" of material within our Solar System have not become sterile or lost over billions of years, and that scientists will still be able to pick up the elusive clues with which they can piece together the story as it actually happened.

Our Solar System is part of an enormous gathering of stars, planets and interstellar matter that is referred to as the Milky Way Galaxy. Our galaxy measures 10,000 to 15,000 light years in extent at its thickest point, and is about 100,000 light years in diameter. It resembles a huge automobile tire with the hub cap in place.

Moving out from the hub about three fourths of the way to the extreme edge is our Sun—30,000 light years from the center of the galaxy. It can be seen as a faintly glowing yellow star, and not really a very impressive star as stars go. Once every 200 million years, the Sun (and our Solar System) makes one complete revolution round the hub of the galaxy in an established orbit. Meanwhile, the Milky Way Galaxy is also constantly turning in space. It is composed of stars, gases, star- and gas-clouds, and other stellar matter which can be seen from Earth on a clear night as a faint stream of wispy white.

The distances in the galaxy are staggering even to try to comprehend. To make the universe even more challenging to comprehend, there are hundreds (even thousands) of other galaxies that astronomers have seen through telescopes. The Earth, then, as a small planet in a Solar System which is part of a common galaxy in one tiny corner of the universe, is small enough to humble any of us. To carry this thought a little farther, scientists in 1959 began a mighty assault on space that required the greatest combined efforts

Jupiter, photographed in blue light through the giant 200-inch Hale Telescope. Its large Red Spot is clearly visible.

of Earth's finest minds and all they have learned—and we only reached the Moon.

Such an awesome expanse does not daunt scientists, though, because they are bent upon the most incredible scientific crusade in the history of civilization. Scientists have long been engaged in a system of thoughtful investigation of the world (and the universe), which is known as the scientific method. With the computer to help, to solve mathematical problems in fractions of a second that formerly took months to figure out, astronauts have been sent into space—an achievement that was not possible 20 years ago.

The Planets: Stepping Stones to Space

It is difficult to realize that science has barely begun to explore space. Because the march to the Moon was amazingly successful, the planets seem very close at hand to many scientists who now want those same methods to be trained upon Venus and Mars. Although regular manned explorations of the planets will certainly not become a reality until near the turn of the century, or about the year 2000, scientists understandably think in terms of

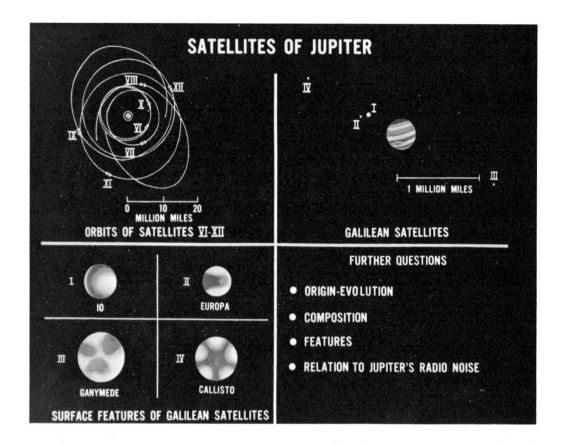

SATELLITES OF JUPITER

ORBITS OF SATELLITES VI-XII

0   10   20
MILLION MILES

GALILEAN SATELLITES

1 MILLION MILES

FURTHER QUESTIONS

- ORIGIN-EVOLUTION
- COMPOSITION
- FEATURES
- RELATION TO JUPITER'S RADIO NOISE

I — IO
II — EUROPA
III — GANYMEDE
IV — CALLISTO

SURFACE FEATURES OF GALILEAN SATELLITES

moving out beyond our Solar System. As they acquire knowledge with each new exploration, they will continually want to reach out farther and farther— each time extending the limits of mechanical and human endurance. The instruments and the spacecraft being built now to investigate the planets are still very much in the "Wright brothers" stage of aeronautical technology.

When scientists become capable of conquering the planets and astronauts travel from place to place within our own Solar System, the planets may be used as stepping stones to other galaxies. By then, astronauts will have to be travelling in spacecraft that move at the speed of light. Even so, they will still be only on the brink of the frontier of space exploration.

The obvious purpose of scientific technology is that it be used for the benefit of mankind. Knowledge merely for the sake of knowledge is relatively valueless unless it can be used to accomplish some purpose. Discovering the principle of the lever enabled people to move things from one place to another; discovering steam led men to invent engines. By applying the knowledge obtained by exploring the planets and the Sun, scientists and engineers may be able to invent new machines, cure crippling diseases, create new fabrics, hopefully improve the agricultural productivity of resources not only on Earth but also on other planets, and perhaps find out how matter is created.

Developing and improving the capability of the Space Shuttle craft, the space "work horse" of the future, is the key to successful investigation of the planets and the Solar System. The Shuttle will carry personnel and, even more important in the beginning, also satellites and photo-reconnaissance spacecraft. Streaking through space at a high speed, the Shuttle will be able to reach the vicinity of Jupiter or Uranus to launch several satellites which will then orbit round the planet.

On another level, the Space Shuttle will help bring about the in-space building of Baseline Space Stations anywhere in our Solar System, will help in the rotation of their crews, supply men and supplies to different planetary bases, and will conduct a variety of specialized missions designed to explore scientifically the contents of the Solar System. This type of sophistication may very well become a reality by the year 2000.

Saturn, photographed in 1969 by a 61-inch telescope from Arizona in the ultra-violet (UV), blue (B) and infrared (IR) regions of the spectrum, reveals a considerable presence in the atmosphere of the chemical methane (dark regions in each picture). The image marked M was taken in the wavelength of methane, leaving light the non-methane areas. South is at the top of each photo.

These three photos of Uranus, overexposed to show its satellites, were taken by an 82-inch telescope in Arizona. Uranus has five "moons."

A Space Shuttle with nuclear capability—a craft of advanced design and able to travel at great speeds—will open up exploration of the Solar System on a vast, rewarding scale. A network of orbiting space stations, space bases and interplanetary satellites for communication and technological application will be serviced by several Shuttle craft which will flit from planet to planet and never touch Earth for as long as several years at a time. With this capability, Solar System exploration will enter a new era and the space science community will have at its command the tools to conquer the Solar System on an unlimited basis.

There is no reason why astronauts on the Shuttle will not be able to retrieve orbiting samples from the Asteroid Belt and carry them either to Earth, to laboratories on the Moon, or to a science laboratory on Mars. By the time this is feasible, say, about 2000, scientists will have built into satellites and reconnaissance spacecraft a new concept of technology under which modular instruments could be removed from them *without interrupting their orbits*. A meteorological satellite in orbit round Jupiter, for instance, would be approached by a Shuttle; a space technician would float over to it and retrieve film packs or micro-meteoroid strike detectors, replace the old instrument with a new one, and carry the precious cargo back to the Shuttle, which will then zip it to the nearest planetary laboratory or space station for study.

The types of activities just described will be speeded up immeasurably by increased development of the Space Shuttle's capability, and that of course is a primary goal. As soon as that capability becomes a reality, astronauts will be ready to leave the Solar System and explore farther into space. While we do not yet know where precisely they will go or what they will find, the anticipation of both is an exciting adventure in creative imagination. The world's best telescopes so far have provided only a glimmer of what exists even within our own Solar System. What lies beyond could be truly breath-taking!

When we examine a new car for the first time, we sit behind the driver's wheel and try out all the instruments, check the heating and air-conditioning systems, adjust the seat this way or that, start up the engine and get "the feel of the car" as an object. After that, we raise the hood and take a long look at the engine and all the other paraphernalia associated with it, examine the tires and the rest of the car's exterior. To get a better understanding of what the car will do, we "test drive" it for manoeuvrability, speed, braking and steering ability. But before we buy a car, we first stand off at a distance and study it in comparison with all the other cars we know about. This comparison is essential, and may be the deciding factor in our purchase.

Ideally, scientists will follow the same process in examining the Space Shuttle and the Solar System. Eventually, they must stand off from both at a distance to get a real understanding of what the total adventure is likely to entail. To explore it all requires a spacecraft of exceptionally high speed because of the great distances. A team of specialized space scientists travelling at the speed of light would only be able to journey half way to the nearest stars, Proxima and Alpha Centauri, in about two years. But from such a vantage point in space, our Solar System would begin to take shape as a grouping of planets. What these scientists would discover in the course of their journey is anyone's guess, but they would begin to see how the Solar

This photo of Uranus was taken by a three-ton, 36-inch telescope carried aloft to 80,400 feet by the unmanned observation balloon Stratoscope II in 1970.

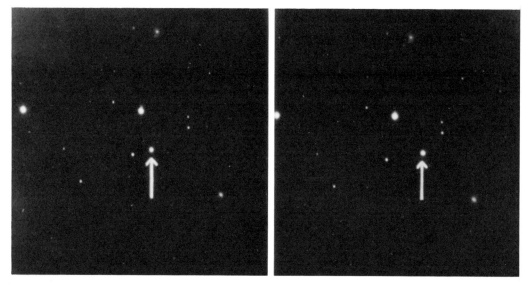

Because of its immense distance from Earth (3,680,000,000 miles), Pluto appears tiny in our telescopes, but actually is about as big as Mars. It was not discovered until 1930 as a planet, because its orbit around the Sun takes 248 years.

System relates to our galaxy and to the other objects and phenomena within that galaxy.

Scientists and engineers are vitally concerned with conquering the obstacles of distance and time; they must find a way to shorten one of these factors. Since they cannot bring the universe closer, they must learn how to move about within it in a shorter amount of time. While they are working to develop high-speed abilities in space, they do not yet know how much pressure, knocking about, physical inactivity or psychological abuse the human body can withstand; biological studies over the next several decades will give them the answer. Finding those answers, however, takes time and careful scientific testing.

By the year 2000, it is hoped that communication in space will have reached a high level of sophistication—enough to enable astronauts in the vicinity of Neptune and Pluto to communicate directly with scientists on Earth both vocally and by means of picture images. The laser is expected to be highly perfected by then. Scientists may also have used the laser to create a new and more promising communication method. Perhaps Pluto will have a set of manned orbital Space Stations and reconnaissance satellites from which information will be sent across the Solar System in streams. And by then perhaps astronauts will be looking forward to "the big one"—the first manned expedition beyond Pluto, out into the infinite stretches of extra-planetary space.

4. TOMORROW IN SPACE

People in everyday walks of life (the proverbial "men on the street") are familiar with the Moon, the Sun, some of the planets (especially Mars), and the fact that we live in a vaguely measurable area known as the Universe. This understanding is woefully inadequate for thinking of the future in space. To begin with, we cannot measure the Universe—in fact, some scientists are convinced that our "universe" is only a small part of a greater whole, and that there may well be *an infinite number of universes*.

The galaxy of which we are a part (the Milky Way) measures roughly 100,000 light years from end to end. Astronomers have already found several dozen galaxies "close by" us ranging in size from 70,000 to 700,000 light years in diameter. There are actually millions of galaxies in the vicinity of our universe, and each galaxy contains millions upon millions of "suns" similar to our own. Beyond these are billions of other galaxies each measuring close to 70,000 to 700,000 light years in diameter. It is far too vast an idea for the average person to understand to the point of accepting it.

Probably the greatest problem in understanding space lies in our own attitudes and beliefs. We may not completely understand the concept of infinite space because this locates man as a tiny speck in an awesome universe where he has no possible significance at all. Human pride is just not prepared to come to terms with this shattering realization. We may not be able to really accept what space is until we have reached a higher level of human maturity. In order to deal effectively with space and all that it promises and implies, we shall have to put away any pride or childish notions about man's importance and learn to be thinking, rational, purposeful human beings.

This book, up to this point, has been devoted to the terribly confining principles of space exploration in our own Solar System and in a time period extending only to about the year 2000. These are convenient concepts, however, and certainly must be understood before we can begin talking about extragalactic theory and interstellar space travel. We cannot, though, accept for a single minute the belief that this is all of what we call space. We have been awed by astronauts on the Moon, photographic spacecraft to the planets, and the exciting ideas of weekly travel by Shuttle to our Moon and to Mars. But this still is not all of what is meant by space exploration.

Our island Earth, photographed from 22,300 miles in space.

One of the most vital terms in the space exploration vocabulary is the word *capability*, meaning the physical, psychological and technological ability to perform work in space. Man has the capability of landing an expedition on some mythical planet in an as yet unknown galaxy in some remote place in the universe. *But man cannot yet travel to that far place.* The capability of the Apollo 11 crew's landing on the Moon is comparable to prehistoric man's sudden realization that by straddling a floating log he can move himself from one shore to another. That's about where we stand today in space exploration.

Unfortunately (or fortunately) man's brain works faster than his hands, and his hands move faster than his emotions. This has created a set of "lags" that often are severe obstacles. Space scientists envision a miraculous future in space exploration, but can only build the equipment to carry out these visions at a certain slow pace. Once the instruments are built, the scientists must not only teach people to accept them and their application to commercial purposes, but must also convince the people in government that such instruments are worthwhile, useful and able to lift the human race to a new and better life style. The first lag is called "technological lag" and the second, "social lag."

Scientists, with their sights on the future, are continuing to establish new theories to prove or disprove. They will continue to reach for the stars, but work to lay a precise and proper groundwork that will serve as proven experience for future space scientists to draw upon. Now is the time to allow scientists to perform their creative thinking with the full and unrestrained freedom they deserve. Our present limitations in space are only temporary.

Ferry Boats in Space

Among the Space Stations, Lunar and Martian Surface Bases, satellites and manned spacecraft, another basic unit besides the Space Shuttle is still needed to carry out the duties of just plain working in space. The Shuttle, as we have seen, will become the primary work horse of travel in near space— to the Moon, the planets, and in transporting equipment and placing satellites in orbit. The task of repair/maintenance of orbiting equipment, where the Shuttle is too large, too fast and too cumbersome to be practical, will have to be done by a much different type of craft.

Space scientists have seized upon the manned Ferry Boat or Space Tug as an economical, useful carrier of men with hammers and pliers in their hands to fix malfunctioning satellites. The Space Tug is intended to operate on the same principle as the Lunar Landing Module of the Apollo program, having the Moon (or a planet) as its home base. From here, it can take off and rocket itself to a rendezvous with an orbiting craft. Astronaut/engineers will be able to leave the Tug to float over to the errant craft, repair broken or non-

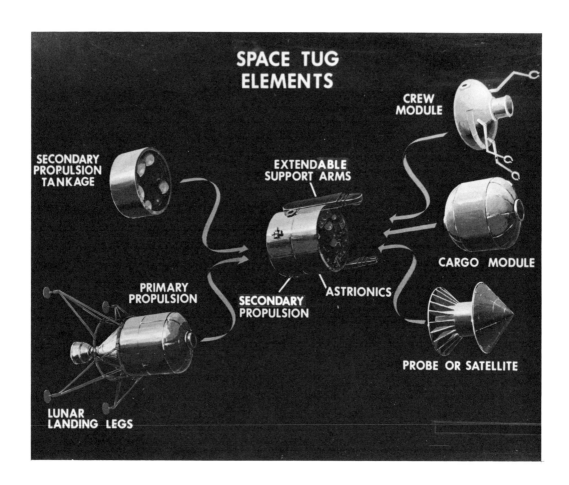

SPACE TUG ELEMENTS

SECONDARY PROPULSION TANKAGE

CREW MODULE

EXTENDABLE SUPPORT ARMS

CARGO MODULE

PRIMARY PROPULSION

SECONDARY PROPULSION

ASTRIONICS

PROBE OR SATELLITE

LUNAR LANDING LEGS

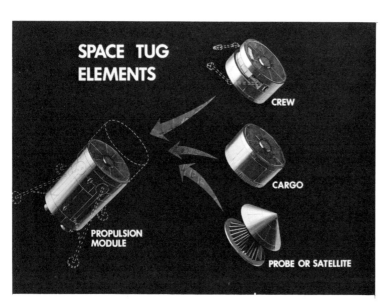

SPACE TUG ELEMENTS

CREW

CARGO

PROPULSION MODULE

PROBE OR SATELLITE

The multi-moduled Space Tug is most useful for repair and maintenance missions and short-duration flights. This diagram shows how different parts of the Tug concept fit together.

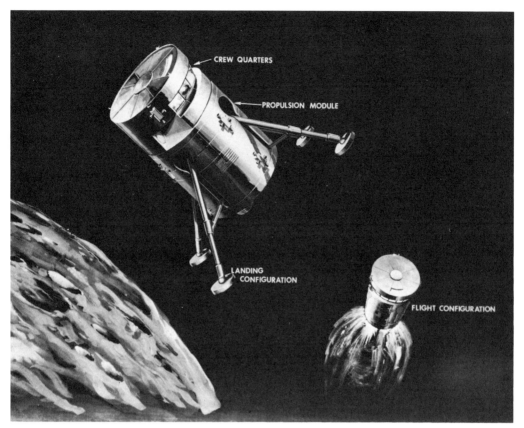

CREW QUARTERS

PROPULSION MODULE

LANDING CONFIGURATION

FLIGHT CONFIGURATION

How the Space Tug would be used on Moon missions. Versatility is the Tug's main value.

functioning systems, retrieve or exchange film packs from an orbiting telescope, for example, or even hook onto an orbiting craft and tow it into another orbit or pull it closer to an orbiting space station for extended repairs.

Some Space Tugs and Ferry Boats may have an orbiting space station for a home base so they can be operated by crews of maintenance personnel as part of their normal work duties. By tying a broken-down satellite to a Space Station, engineers will be able to float back and forth between the two craft making long-term changes or repairs with a minimum of danger and lost time. If necessary, the astronauts in a Tug may bring the satellite back to a central repair station on the lunar surface, land and make the necessary repairs, and then carry the satellite back up into orbit.

The value of the Space Tug will be in prolonging by repair the life of already-orbiting satellites, thereby reducing the cost of having to replace a whole satellite because one part of it is not operating properly. As a working unit, the Tug will very quickly "earn its way" in the space program not only by drastically reducing costs, but also by cutting down the time required for specific activities.

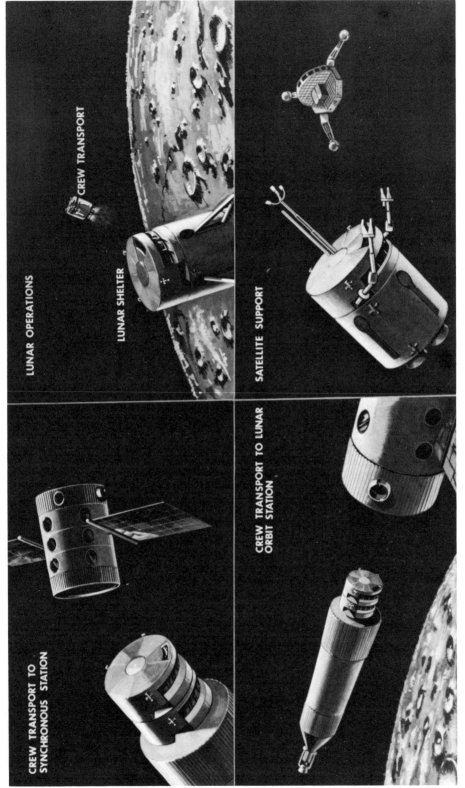

CREW TRANSPORT TO SYNCHRONOUS STATION

LUNAR OPERATIONS

CREW TRANSPORT

LUNAR SHELTER

CREW TRANSPORT TO LUNAR ORBIT STATION

SATELLITE SUPPORT

Some uses of the Space Tug with its Crew Module.

The Space Tug Crew Module has a pair of grappling arms to assemble components in space, or perhaps to manipulate large objects, such as retrieving an errant or malfunctioning satellite.

Plans are already under consideration to place several kinds of work modules in space. One would be a Telescope Module whose task would be controlled from the ground, the Moon or an orbiting Space Station. A number of these telescopes are needed for separate purposes, but mainly they depend upon use of photographic films to carry out astronomical research. Most astronomers spend little time looking through telescopes; they study photographs taken through the telescope. The Space Tug would be invaluable in servicing these work modules.

As a general concept the Tug is planned to carry three or four astronauts in a life-support section that is detachable from the engineering/fuel section. The life-support container will carry equipment, tools, steering console and communications, and also a large storage area. In addition it will have two remote-controlled arms that extend outward from the craft to be used while in orbit to clasp or manipulate an object of up to several tons. An airlock/escape hatch will allow free exit and entrance for astronauts. On the sides of the Tug life-support container will be manoeuvring rockets to allow the whole container to navigate itself separately in space. The Space Tug kind of ferry boat can be compared to an Earth tow truck, or "trouble wagon."

It is not always convenient to have to land a spacecraft just to take on more fuel. Presently planned are Orbiting Refueling Tankers, to be placed in permanent orbits round the Moon, the Earth or another planet. These will carry thousands of hours of fuel like a sea-going oil tanker, and will do much to help speed up what otherwise would be an expensive and time-consuming refueling operation. The Orbiting Refueling Tanker would be capable of changing its orbit if necessary, but usually would remain on station

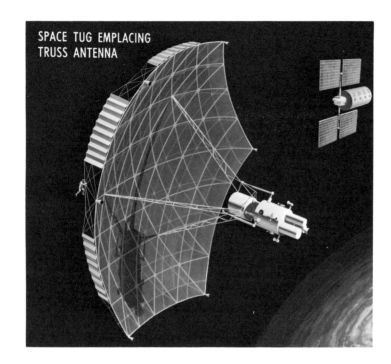

SPACE TUG EMPLACING
TRUSS ANTENNA

This art rendering
shows how the
Space Tug can assist
in placing a large
truss-type antenna
in orbit. The Tug can
handle many times
its own weight.

in "parking orbit" while other craft make their rendezvous with it. Since the bulk of the manned craft (and many unmanned craft) now being planned for space operations in the near future make use of liquid fuel, Orbiting Refueling Tankers will be vitally important.

The Orbiting Tanker can be sent out far ahead of a mission—to be placed in planetary orbit around, say, Mars or Jupiter. Perhaps even a long string of Tankers leading from the Moon to one of the far planets would provide important stopping stations for manned spacecraft voyaging back and forth from planet to planet. The Tankers might have crews to assist in refueling and to resupply life-support materials. A large Tanker in orbit around Jupiter, for example, would become a major way-station to resupply a manned expedition to Saturn with fuel, oxygen, food and other materials.

The Orbiting Refueling Tanker is first envisioned as an enormously long tube fitted with compartments separating fuel, oxygen, etc. The tube doesn't necessarily have to be in a straight line, though. By bending tubes into circles, several of them could be attached together for a really mammoth refueling station that would remain on-station somewhere in space for several years, and then be refueled itself by another Tanker. Crew rotation could be accomplished by Shuttle. The Orbiting Tanker, a filling station in space, would greatly increase the capabilities of all kinds of manned missions.

The Space Tug, Orbiting Refueling Tanker and other Ferry Boats will not be designed for speed; they will be created for specific work purposes which do not necessarily include travelling great distances in a hurry. Still, they could always serve as special emergency stations in which endangered crews could take temporary shelter if a mishap occurred on board their own spacecraft. A manned expedition returning from Jupiter or Saturn would at least have some place to go, or a station to which astronauts could call for help in an emergency.

A Tanker composed of tubes 1,000 yards long (straight or curved) and perhaps 60 feet in diameter would have facilities also for smaller craft, such as a Space Tug or Shuttle Craft, to be docked with it. The smaller craft would be assigned to the Tanker for certain time periods. Such a concept would extend repair and maintenance capabilities literally through the Solar System.

Searching Out the Sun

As the scientists' understanding of the Sun becomes more complete, it will be possible not only to use those newly-discovered principles, but to put the Sun to work for us directly. Scientists know that the Sun is the source of incredible energy. If devices can harness more of that energy and use it to greater advantage, man will have an unlimited source of power close at hand. Present uses of the Sun in exploring space are limited to solar energy cells which convert sunlight into electrical energy for powering satellites and certain kinds of spacecraft, and using the Sun's heat to keep instruments warm in the cold temperatures of space.

The Sun's gases, heated by the furnace beneath, expand and rise from the center irregularly at a rapid rate. This phenomenon is called Solar Wind and its speed of expansion (when active) has been calculated to be about 1 to 2 million miles per hour, or about 300 miles per second. Scientists

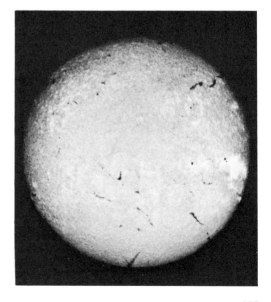

The solar furnace, our own peculiar star, is seen here strewn with solar flares (dark sunspots). This photo was taken by the Solar Particle Alert Network at NASA's Manned Spacecraft Center, Houston, Texas.

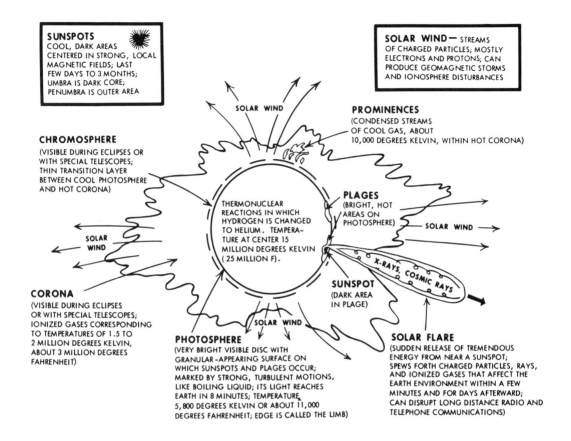

conjecture that certain types of lightweight spacecraft could receive "push" from the Solar Wind much as a sailboat is blown along by the Earth's wind. If true, the Solar Wind could reduce considerably the costs of fuel in spacecraft.

Most of the observations of the Sun, however, have been taken from Earth. Scientists do not yet know the speed of the Solar Wind when and if it reaches Jupiter or Saturn. A spacecraft "blown" out to Jupiter could possibly become marooned if the Wind should die out, and if it did not have any other means of locomotion. At the same time, a Sun-searching satellite could be placed in Solar orbit and possibly kept there by the Solar Wind for an indefinite period, excluding the likelihood of its being burned up by the Sun's heat.

Solar array panels on spacecraft have been planned to use the Sun's rays for powering nuclear reactors, but they could be used for powering low-thrust electric propulsion rockets instead. In another application, the Sun's rays could be used to heat a gas on board a spacecraft and cause it to expand rapidly and continuously. The gas, under pressure, would then be forced through a narrow nozzle, providing a means of propulsion.

Several times a year, a "solar flare" or sunspot erupts on the surface of the Sun and spews out radiation into the Solar System. In large amounts, radiation is deadly to life on our planet, but it can be and has been tolerated in small doses. Scientists are now beginning to believe that radiation is not the danger it once was supposed to be, because it is scattered so widely. If this radiation can be usefully trapped and converted into usable energy, it could possibly supply a means of propulsion.

These sudden and widespread solar flares have periods of extreme activity occurring about every 11 years. Occasionally they disrupt radio communication on Earth. By studying the Sun during these 11-year cycles, scientists have learned a great deal, and if they can study at close range they will certainly learn more. However, the investigation will have to be done by instruments because human tissue cannot withstand such a concentrated bombardment of solar radiation.

Solar array panels the size of several football fields placed side by side in rows on the Moon could provide an endless source of energy and give medium amounts of power to a lunar surface base. Better still, the energy created by the panels could be stored until needed, and might very well provide a source of emergency power on the Moon. Expand this same idea to an area 100 miles square, and the potential uses become even more exciting.

Some scientists believe it possible in the future for astronauts to bounce from star to star by means of solar propulsion entirely, using spacecraft "sails" of enormous size. While such a proposal is thoroughly sound scientifically, it is rarely considered for manned space travel because it is too slow. The theory derives from the fact that sunlight itself exerts pressure on a flat surface, about one ten millionth of a pound per square foot. An extremely thin, highly reflective surface a mile square would receive about five pounds of pressure per square foot. A sail a mile square would not have to weigh a great amount—possibly only 10 or 12 tons, which in orbit would be negligible. A spacecraft fitted with this immense sail could be "pressured" along, gathering momentum and speed as it went, eventually achieving a surprising rate of travel. Science writer Arthur Clarke suggests its speed after one day would be about 500 miles per hour, and after 10 days about 5,000 miles per hour. If this ratio increase were to continue, the craft could theoretically reach the speed of light in a very short time.

Scientists are not so concerned about applying what they know today about the Sun as they are excited about its potential. What they will learn in the next 20 years about the Sun could very well reorganize their whole scheme of scientific thought. The importance of the Sun, therefore, depends upon their

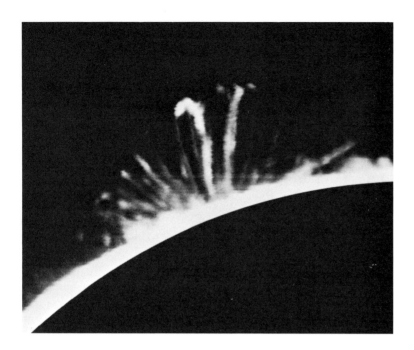

Solar flares erupt as far as 500,000 miles into space.

ability to learn about it and to apply this new knowledge to problem-solving. The Sun, for example, has a mass almost equal to the size of our entire Solar System. A person weighing 100 pounds on Earth would weigh about 2,800 pounds on the Sun. It would require a mighty spaceship to blast off from the Sun's surface. Of course, that is not being considered, but if a spacecraft were to be launched from near the Sun by "slingshot," such a craft could build up a tremendous speed and literally be shot out into the Solar System on a magnificent journey.

Despite the fact that many space probes have returned information about the Sun, and despite the fact that astronomers have studied it for several centuries, scientists still know little about it. Some of the immediate information they need to have is:

☐ What is the exact nature of sunspots, and how do they relate to other phenomena on the Sun?

☐ What causes the 11-year cycle of solar activity?

☐ What causes change in the pattern of the Sun's magnetic field?

☐ How was the Sun, actually a star, originally formed, and is it possible that all other stars or just some of them were formed in the same way?

☐ What causes the enormous solar prominences (seen during eclipses) to erupt on the surface of the Sun?

☐ What is the approximate age of the Sun? How long will it continue to burn?

☐ What is the composition of the various layers of the Sun?

136

☐ Why is the photosphere (the portion that emits light) cooler in temperature (10,472° F or 5,800° C) than the chromosphere and corona which envelope it?

Between the Planets

The asteroids, also called planetoids, located between Mars and Jupiter are contained in a circular belt which itself is constantly in motion round the Sun. Each individual asteroid appears to have its own orbit, most of them nearly circular, a few elliptical. Viewed from deep space, this belt might appear as a loosely-formed string of chunks of material. The chunks range in size from several feet in diameter to as large as about 480 miles across (the planetoid Ceres).

Space scientists believe the asteroids are actually bits of an exploded or disintegrated planet, formed or fractured at the same time our Solar System was created. Very little is known about these asteroids except that they seem to conform to the over-all characteristics and composition of the rest of our Solar System.

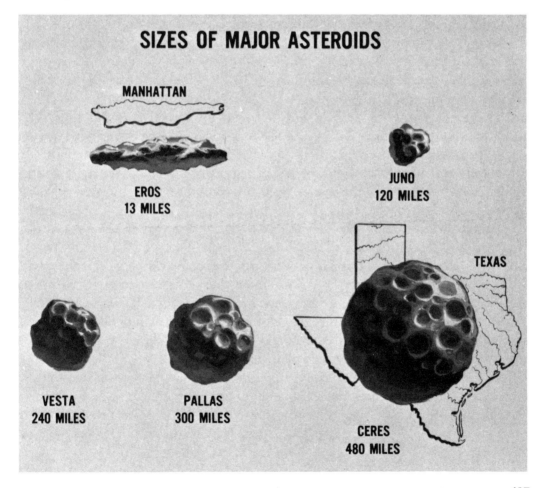

SIZES OF MAJOR ASTEROIDS

MANHATTAN

EROS
13 MILES

JUNO
120 MILES

TEXAS

VESTA
240 MILES

PALLAS
300 MILES

CERES
480 MILES

Scientists believe it is possible to make use of the asteroids, especially the larger ones, in several interesting ways. Of the approximately 1,700 known and charted bigger asteroids, only about 20 are larger than 100 miles in length. It is possible, of course, to mine these asteroids as one would mine any kind of raw material. By using the material gained from them, new and perhaps better products could be created. Mining them is just one plan.

Space scientists in particular have thought of using the asteroids as stopping stations, or as reconnaissance platforms. The floating islands would become interplanetary outposts for relaying communications and for re-bouncing laser beams, or as emergency refuges, astronomical observatories, refueling platforms, or even as tourist areas. Some visionaries have suggested hollowing out the larger asteroids for underground bases where astronauts could spend a tour of duty and conduct research. If the asteroid base were a relay point, it might even hold permanent storage tanks.

The asteroid belt may also be a key to unravelling mysteries about the creation of the Solar System, for they very likely played some kind of a rôle in that formation. Manned missions to Mars and beyond will surely want to stop in the belt region to gather chunks of the smaller asteroids for examination. Scientists need to know the age of these chunks, and if they were all formed at the same time and in the same way. They need to know their composition, and how that composition relates to the rest of the Solar System. It is strange that the belt seems to "hold together" instead of being attracted to one of the nearby planets.

Between the planets is much more material for scientists to examine. For example, scientists believe it is possible for a spacecraft to scoop up some of the interplanetary hydrogen (and maybe helium) for use as a propellant. It is the thin hydrogen gas they are interested in. This could power a fusion ramjet, which would eliminate the need for on-board fuel storage and help reduce the weight of the ship.

Scientists do not really know what is between the planets. Returns from satellites and reconnaissance spacecraft indicate various levels of micro-meteorite bombardment, usually by very tiny particles. Besides that, there are the usual gases and known chemicals in various forms, such as hydrogen, helium, carbon, depending on how near or far the spacecraft is to a planet. Since travel so far has been limited to our Solar System, scientists believe it is time to begin thinking about what is in space beyond Pluto—perhaps it will prove to be another void between planets.

The most difficult obstacle to overcome between the planets is the void of sheer space itself—distance in miles, and in astronomical units. If a manned expedition were to start out to Pluto today, it would take two years to get to Mars, two more to Jupiter, two to Saturn, maybe three to Uranus, two to

Neptune and an additional three years to Pluto. That makes 14 years in all—much too long a time for a team to remain cooped up even in a large space-ship. Imagine having to spend 14 years on a medium-sized yacht, forever sailing the oceans.

It is not easy to figure out how the void between the planets could ever be useful to science, simply because the distances are too great. Still, scientists are slowly learning to refrain from believing that anything is really impossible. Perhaps the interplanetary voids will become populated with man-made spacecraft, stations or even small cities floating eternally like awesome artificial satellites, all having cultures of their own.

The Endless Search for Life

We would be highly egotistical to believe that ours is the only inhabitable planet in the universe, or that ours is the only proper Solar System combination in existence. The star 61 Cygni, about 11 light years away, is a double star whose behavior suggests there is a third body, a planet, moving about it. Barnard's star, 6 light years away, has an object orbiting about it. The star Lalande 21185 has a larger companion circling about it. These are only three quick examples of other star-planet combinations. Many, many stars are doublets and triplets, and astronomers are beginning to believe that single stars without planets are the exception instead of the rule.

Our telescopic equipment is not strong enough to be able to detect many other solar systems in space. This type of scientific research must be left for observatories built on the Moon, or for large telescopes orbiting the Earth where atmosphere does not distort their view. Once convinced that solar systems are as common as stars, scientists realize that there are thousands upon thousands of them in our Milky Way galaxy alone. Considering the billions of observable and suspected stars in our galaxy, it would be the height of ignorance to think for a moment that our Sun is the only star with a planetary system.

Scientists are careful in settling upon a definition of what is called "life." Naturally, people from Earth tend to think of life in space as something akin to life forms on Earth. Plant life and animal life, of course, are possibilities on planets having water and an atmosphere. But when we talk about the possibility of finding life in space, generally we mean intelligent life.

Talking to another species or race, if one exists, is presently being attempted. For years, giant transmitters have been sending out radio messages daily and listening for replies: Where are you? Who are you? Here I am. I exist. Do you hear me?

At the same time, a staff is actively engaged in listening—to learn if anyone out there is trying to contact us. Language is not really the problem, because any other intelligent race capable of receiving our message or of returning it will certainly be highly educated in mathematics, the common universal language. To build their own equipment for interstellar communication, they would have to be at least as far advanced as we are, and they might even be more advanced.

If we sent a message out to the most populated regions in space in 1972, it is possible we could not get an answer from a planet in another solar system light years away for many years, since the process of communication must pass a considerable distance in two directions, need to be deciphered, etc. Our grandchildren or grandchildren's grandchildren might be the recipients of the return message.

What are we going to talk about? Our first message should contain a great deal of information in order to save time. Dr. Frank D. Drake once sent his colleagues in astronomy and physics a message on paper that was nothing more than a series of ones and zeros typed in a long continuous line. It was, he said, the kind of message to outer space that would have considerable meaning to anyone intelligent enough to receive it. The message had a total of 1271 digits. Since the number 1271 is the product of two prime numbers, 31 and 41, receivers could arrange the digits in two ways—two different grids of 31 and 41 lines respectively. One of the grids (vertical arrangement of 41 lines) produces nothing, but the other (31 lines down, 41 lines across) discloses a picture-message that is absolutely unmistakable when the ones are shaded in.

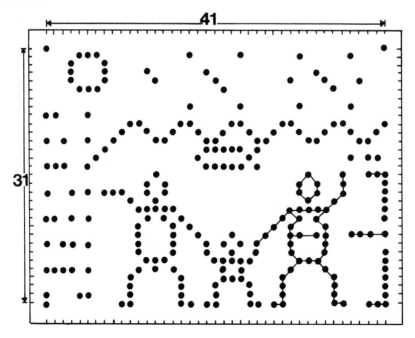

If someone on Earth were to send such a message, it would be transmitted most efficiently at the universally understood frequency of 1,420 megacycles per second. That frequency has a rather short wavelength of 21 centimeters and even amid all the "radio noise" in space would stand out like a red light. But to send such a message *just once* aimed at each of the most highly populated regions of the universe would take decades of time even if 1,000 transmitters were used, which is of course economically prohibitive. The sender would probably not get an answer within his own lifetime.

Sending signals by radio presumes that the receiver is capable of hearing. Actually, according to the evolution of life forms and the physical properties of living creatures, *seeing* is a more universal sense. It would be far more productive to transmit a picture because chances are that other creatures in the universe will be able to see much better than they can hear. Perhaps we are wasting our time trying to send radio signals when we should be building giant television transmitters.

Do we really want to get an answer from someone out there? The answer is an unqualified, Yes! Other creatures in space may have developed much more sophisticated means of sending messages. Certainly 100 years from now will find man using a more capable instrument than radio or television. Perhaps by then we will be transmitting images by laser or have adopted a method we cannot even dream of now.

There is life out in space because logic suggests it cannot be otherwise. Some day (100 years, perhaps 500 years from now) we will encounter other life forms, and establish some sort of communication. Hopefully, at such a time, we will be mature enough to accept a relationship with people of another solar system. It is the height of conceit for us to believe that another species of life from another planet would want to conquer us, as science fiction writers tend to think. What could we possibly offer a race of beings who travelled to our little Earth and saw our feeble, tribal customs? Surely they would consider us primitive and most likely unfit for their association.

The prospect of communicating with other beings, or of finding them, forces us to realize that as searchers in the universe we come from an infinitisimally small corner of the cosmos which is possibly billions of years younger than the other planets. To accomplish such an encounter, we are going to have to be much more advanced technically and psychologically than we are now.

One of the most intriguing thoughts on communication in space was actually carried out by Cornell University astronomers Carl Sagan and Frank Drake—a metal plaque fastened to the Pioneer F spacecraft to Jupiter (now designated Pioneer 10 by NASA). The craft was launched in February, 1972, and, after passing Jupiter, will swing out into space to travel until it dis-

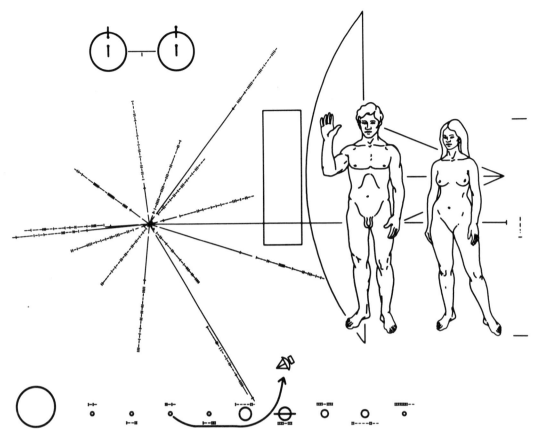

The metal plaque fastened to the Pioneer 10 spacecraft headed for Jupiter may fall into the hands of intelligent beings, and these symbols are intended, without words, to convey information about the Earth and its people.

integrates. Space scientists estimate it would take 80,000 years for the little craft to reach our nearest star.

If the craft is seized by another race from another planet, it will tell them an amazing amount of information about the place from which it came. The symbols contained on the plaque can be readily understood by anyone unfamiliar with Earth forms. It bears representations of Man, Woman, Solar System, Earth (showing the craft was launched here), an atom of hydrogen which is the most abundant chemical in the universe, and a large starburst pattern symbolizing pulsars, distance from end to end of our galaxy, and our use of the 21-centimeter wavelength in radio communication.

Some of the other features are fascinating, too. The height of the Earth people is compared to the size of the Pioneer craft itself to give an indication of the size of Earthlings. The hydrogen atom's pulse of radiation on the plaque is indicated at 21 centimeters, the basic unit of measurement of the plaque.

An intelligent creature in space, understanding the concept of 21 centimeters, could very quickly switch its radio gear to the 1,420 megacycles and instantly probe to pick up our radio transmissions.

To the right of the woman is the binary symbol for 8, which when multiplied by 21 centimeters gives the height of the woman as 5½ feet. The message not only denotes that the Pioneer craft left from the third planet from the Sun, but that it shot past the fifth (Jupiter) and then swept out into space. The plaque measures a scant 6 inches by 9 inches and is made of aluminum anodized with erosion-resistant gold, which in itself will tell something of the manufactured material produced on our planet. We can imagine the excitement of other beings if and when they find Pioneer and its message, by realizing how we would react to receiving such a message ourselves in the same way.

If we search in vain for intelligent life, there is always the possibility of starting our own on some other planet and building a whole new culture. Some suggestions have already been made for "seeding" a planet like Venus or Jupiter with Earth life forms that conceivably will survive and begin the same kind of natural chain reaction that started up life on Earth. In such a project, Jupiter may prove to be far more habitable than either Mars or Venus. As for putting human life on another planet, that may be quite another thing until we strengthen our capabilities.

It is not impossible, however, that the 22nd century will see our Solar System populated with artificial floating cities of 200 or 300 square miles orbiting about the Sun and the planets, or even beyond. Such satellite cities would have to be completely self-sustaining, with waste virtually non-existent.

Beyond 2000

The year 2000 by our calendar, now less than 30 years away, has been adopted by some space scientists and sociologists as a kind of milestone in the exploration of space. At the turn of the century, though, we will still be in the most primitive stages of discovery and exploration even if we have established large bases on the Moon and small bases on Mars. Will that year mark the beginning of a new era in which mankind breaks free of the Solar System? If our technology continues to expand geometrically with each new discovery and each new year as it has done since 1900, we may well reach Proxima Centauri, 4.3 light years away, by the year 2100.

A short 300 years back, the microscope was just being invented. And only 400 years ago, Copernicus startled the world by having the temerity to announce that the Earth was no longer the center of the universe, an idea which blasted apart the medieval concepts of astronomy and philosophy!

While "civilization" has progressed, science has advanced still more rapidly.

Even more astonishing, the first several artificial satellites were launched in 1957/1958, and about 10 years later, the first astronauts walked across the surface of the Moon. Is there any doubt that scientists are capable of accomplishing the projects planned for the decades between now and the year 2000?

Men and women must not only colonize the Moon, but must populate it. They must renovate it entirely for their use, which includes large cities and unending means of transportation. A hundred years from now, the Moon should be a second Earth (with some obvious reservations) with railways, subways, airports, swimming pools, air-tight domed villages and mammoth underground, life-stabilizing caverns used for living and production centers. The Moon will be made to pay for itself by mineral mining, astronomical and space-flight research, and the discovery of new combinations of natural materials which will help produce new tools and lead to further inventions.

Astronauts and engineers could be encamped securely on Mars by 2000. Scientists say they have the capability to do it in the next five years! But at the rate that analysts are working, it will take another decade for them to understand the returns from the trip Mariner 9 made to Mars in 1971–72. In fact, men may land on Mars before the scientists fully know what it is they have discovered by the unmanned flights. Once they get to Mars, astronauts could begin to expand human abilities to survive and endure there. Since the planet is nearly fully mapped already by means of Mariner spacecraft, A.D. 2000 may find scientists starting to chart the boundaries of cities and villages, with a view to transporting families to the planet in the first few decades following. Scientists may have explored the Sun and the Solar System rather thoroughly by then, using unmanned spacecraft.

Beyond 2000, man may become so different from man in the 1970's there may be no possible way to compare them. Man living in a space suit much of the time, shuttling in a gravity-less vehicle is different enough to start with. The entire culture of the Earth will be changed, and the other worlds men establish and maintain in space will develop cultures of their own that may be far different from that of Earth.

We may be, as some scientists suggest, truly tending towards a state of Earth unification through common interests in space. If this meeting and melting of present nations and geographical regions into one can be accomplished, this would be a big help to the space program. The United States and the U.S.S.R. are already exchanging technical information about space flights and craft. They have, in fact, also agreed to join forces in space, probably in 1975.

Scientists and others presently engaged in the business of expanding man's horizons in space are beginning to believe that the greatest problem in space travel and exploration is not overcoming the problems imposed by

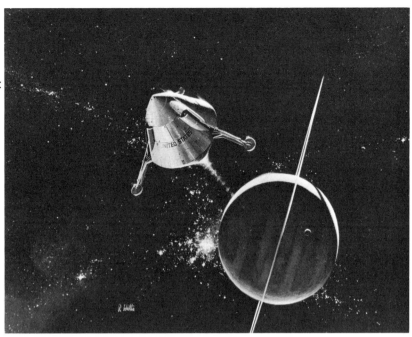

Artist's concept of a futuristic spacecraft.

physics, but rather overcoming man's own biological frailties. Space exploration then becomes not a matter of simply physical laws, but biological ones.

Space exploration can only succeed when science and especially medicine begin to focus all their resources upon the same goals. The cliché that *hard work is a good cure for anything* will never be more true than in the future when mankind needs to knuckle down to its adventures in space. This means gathering together the combined might and skills of scientific thought and physical stamina and endurance to create a stronger human being and faster space ships.

Today we can envision, as writer Arthur Clarke and artist Robert McCall did in the MGM motion picture *2001: A Space Odyssey*, reaching the Moon by speeding starship, spending our time on a satellite way station, and then embarking upon a journey that will take us to Jupiter. Even more exciting, we may see in the 21st century a Moon criss-crossed with nuclear-powered monorail trains flitting back and forth from crater-city to crater-city, carrying people in shirt-sleeve environments, stopping at stations along the way, completing a 500-mile journey in less than a half hour. Dotted here and there over the surface of the Moon may be airports to be visited by types of spacecraft which we can now only scarcely imagine.

Highways constructed from lunar materials may be used by electrically- or atomically-powered vehicles, entirely airtight and guided by computers so there is no need for a driver. These are planned to carry passengers to whatever site they choose to go without their having to wear bulky space suits. The Moon may be a busy place indeed, for all these travellers would live and work here, vitally engaged in the work of pushing man's horizons still farther out into space, and discovering the secrets of the Solar System.

What the people on Earth have learned in the last few millennia may be totally dwarfed by what men will discover and learn in space between the years 2000 and 2099. Scientists expect to harness new energies, discover new materials and laws of nature, find new worlds to explore, travel great distances to see new and amazing phenomena—and most important—build man's stamina to an entirely new level of endurance, physically and emotionally.

No one can afford to be too idealistic about our future in space, unless he knows where and how to obtain the hard cash to pay for it. NASA and the legislators who want the program to continue will have to justify it to the taxpayers on a coldly economic basis. It is uniquely unfortunate that scientifically talented creative people have to stop and take the time to justify a worthwhile idea or invention in terms of material benefits versus money expended. NASA already could build a bridge to the Moon and back out of the memorandums already written as justifications and petitions for financial appropriations from the U.S. Congress.

Launch into the Future

Simply to build a spacecraft and launch it into space, aimed at some distant star, is important enough, but not so important as when a man rides in it. He can live only so long, and survive his loneliness only up to a certain limit. Before an astronaut can be placed on a distant planet, he must be trained and conditioned to survive, since the design or velocity of the spacecraft cannot be altered immediately to accommodate man with his present weaknesses.

Some scientists have suggested developing a man capable of suspended animation. A 30-year-old astronaut launched toward the Andromeda Galaxy in the year 2000, frozen in a life-supporting embryo of protective fluid, could conceivably awaken at Andromeda still only 30 years old, although the trip might take more than 100 calendar years. Experiments with suspended animation indicate that scientists think such a process is possible. It is conceivable that a certain drug or temperature-reduction process like a quick freeze might enable travellers to endure a long period of human hibernation, which could be repeated on the return trip. Imagine what the world would think of these ageless survivors from a long and distant journey—survivors who would land on an Earth that had aged 200 years during their absence.

Another approach to overcoming the problem of travelling great distances requires great determination. A small city could be launched on board a

146

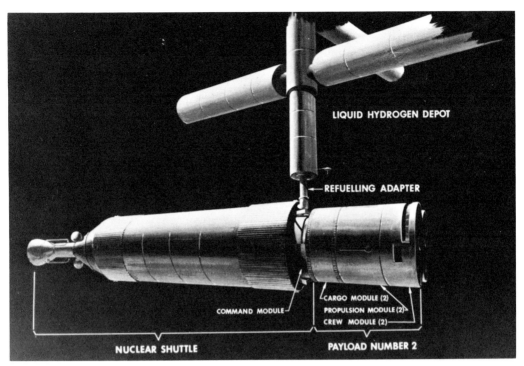

LIQUID HYDROGEN DEPOT

REFUELLING ADAPTER

CARGO MODULE (2)
PROPULSION MODULE (2)
CREW MODULE (2)

COMMAND MODULE

NUCLEAR SHUTTLE   PAYLOAD NUMBER 2

How a nuclear spacecraft refuels from an Orbiting Tanker or fuel depot.

hermetically sealed spaceship into space, loaded with citizens who would be doomed to spend their lives on the ship, give birth to a new generation which would automatically be taught the technology and philosophy of what they are doing, and so eventually bring the spaceship to a successful landing—and return. This is a great deal to ask of people, however, but could be accomplished.

Failing this method, it is also possible to equip a spaceship on a journey of 100 years, for example, with robots and totally-automated systems, including carefully protected containers of artificial insemination ingredients. After the spaceship had travelled for many years, the automatic robots would be triggered to induce the breeding process on board, and produce from the containers a group of healthy babies that would be taught the knowledge and cultural values of the parent civilization back on Earth, and trained to continue the mission.

Upon reaching their destination, they would report everything they found to shipboard computers and memory banks, conduct photographic reconnaissance, and then head for home. If any of the travellers reached the end of their lives during the flight, it would not matter as the automatic robots would take over and either steer the ship back to Earth or raise yet another generation of humankind to be taught to land the ship.

While these methods at first glance seem barbaric or at best highly drastic, they would accomplish the venture and allow men to bring back the information from other solar systems and galaxies. Humans are needed for such missions because automated systems can only accomplish a limited

Radio waves from the outermost fringes of the universe can be received by this radio-telescope near Canberra, Australia. Each of its two intersecting arms is a mile long.

This Teltrac antenna, located at Cape Kennedy, is rotated to aid in communicating with spacecraft, among other functions.

amount in the way of information-gathering. At the same time, such measures require a culture that would ignore the social values that rule at present. Actually though, some segments of American and European society are beginning to accept and inculcate attitudes and beliefs of a public-good nature that would logically lead to such methods becoming morally and ethically approved in a surprisingly short time if left to their own direction.

Western cultures have traditionally placed a high value on human life and are not now receptive to artificial development of humanoid forms for the simple purpose of gaining scientific knowledge. At the same time, the leaders of these cultures might prove to be the leaders in the future of the type of cultural and sociological revolution that could make such methods a reality. If imaginative books like *Brave New World* and *1984* can emerge from the Western culture and appeal to the general public, there is little doubt that people will continue to think about these subjects.

When anyone contemplates the problems of space travel involving multiple light years based on the velocities of present spacecraft, or even the velocities envisioned for tomorrow in space, he finds he must accept the fact that such travel will have to be undertaken by more than one generation of astronaut groups, and in some cases whole populations. He must also accept the fact that the group that leaves will never be heard of or seen again on Earth. Their particular function in the chain of tasks is simply to guide their ship out into space, and plan at a later time for their children to take over. Eventually these children will pass control of the mission to their children in turn.

As capabilities increase, and spaceships are able to travel faster and faster, time and distance will shorten and fewer generations of pilots and explorers will be needed to complete the missions. We might also envision sending out streams of spaceships to colonize the Solar System and beyond, all containing groups of settlers to travel across space until they find a suitable landing place to start their new colony. Assuming some of these many groups evolve their own peculiar way of life and culture, it is possible that some day in the distant future the Earth would be visited by a spaceship from an outside-the-Solar-System colony that developed from a group of explorers originally sent out from Earth or from the Moon.

As our technology increases, one plan is to colonize natural satellites like Jupiter's Ganymede or Saturn's Titan. These colonies in turn then can learn how to survive on the parent planets. The end result would be almost total colonization of the planets and natural satellites in our Solar System. When will we be ready to march out into our galaxy? Some day far beyond to-morrow in space, we may be spreading the human species to galaxies and planets beyond our own tiny Milky Way.

Exploring the Galaxies

As man's knowledge of astronomy, given tremendous impetus by new discoveries in space science, begins to increase and expand, scientists will ultimately arrive at a system of cataloguing the contents of the universe. The heavens seem to be filled with objects having an apparent natural arrangement from very small to very large.

At the smallest end of the universal continuum, besides the asteroids, are the natural satellites of the planets—or moons (some of these may be bigger than Mercury). Next in size are the planets themselves, then the Solar System and our Sun (a star), then the galaxy (the Milky Way), and finally the profusion of galaxies, nebulae, star clusters and star fields we know as the Universe. But scientists are beginning to feel the word "universe" is no longer sufficient to describe the vastness of space.

All the objects that can be seen with a telescope (the Mount Wilson Observatory 200-inch Hale Telescope reaches at least 10,000,000,000 light years out into space) have come to be lumped under the one category *universe*, but there is every reason to believe that all this material still represents merely a tiny speck in one tiny corner of a remote part of a greater whole that has been labelled *The Cosmos*. Some day as our field of view is further widened, scientists might need to coin a word describing something far less limited than The Cosmos.

In all this incredibly and incomprehensibly enormous area, there must be millions upon millions of Solar Systems and billions and billions of other planets. Beyond the straining eyes of our finest telescopes other galaxies are likely to be as numerous as the grains of sand on a beach. Why should we

The 200-inch Hale reflecting telescope at Mount Palomar, California, is one of the largest telescopes on Earth. The observer sits in a little cage inside the circular tube at upper left, near the top of the picture.

suppose then that the Earth is the only stronghold of intelligence in so vast a space? Is it utter nonsense and arrogance?

After men of the 24th or 25th century have thoroughly explored the Milky Way with their incredible machines, they may find themselves ready and eager to press onward to the many other galaxies and star fields that, by then, still stretch beyond the fullest limit of man's endurance. They will be using yardsticks to communicate distances that are not yet within our realm of experience. We can try to comprehend these distances now, just for fun.

A light year (the distance light can travel in a year) is approximately 6,000,000,000,000 miles (called 6 trillion in the U.S.). Proxima Centauri is only 4.3 light years away; that is, it is 4.3 times 6 trillion. This is our closest star. To comprehend space, next try to realize that the Milky Way Galaxy has a diameter of 100,000 light years (from end to end) and it is only an average galaxy. That diameter written out is 600,000,000,000,000,000 miles.

Our Milky Way Galaxy, astronomers tell us, is part of a much larger galaxy called a *supergalaxy*, which as yet has not been determined, let alone measured. The Mount Wilson telescope can reach out about a distance of 10,000,000,000 light years. If we multiply that number by the speed of light (6 trillion) that is the extent into the near universe into which the human eye can now reach. Written, that number is 60,000,000,000,000,000,000,000 miles. At that point, we have reached the veil of space. Beyond lies the rest of our universe, and the Cosmos stretching on (without end?). The 200-inch Hale telescope, if erected on the Moon, would be unencumbered by any kind of atmosphere and would be able to peer perhaps a thousand times that far, which is interesting but still relatively inconsequential.

(Left) Launched in 1971, this NASA Aerobee rocket carried two polarimeters to measure the X-ray polarization of the Crab Nebula. It was the forerunner of much more advanced scientific instruments planned for study of distant stars, nebulae, and galaxies. (Right) Artist's concept of the 120-inch Manned Orbiting Astronomical Telescope being suggested for NASA by the Boeing Company.

Launching a spaceship at a target 60,000,000,000,000,000,000,000 miles in space seems now a colossal undertaking, and certainly it is. By the 25th century, man's attitudes and goals may have changed appreciably.

An Archeologist in Space

Stated in the simplest of terms, the primary task of an archeologist is to locate and examine evidence of past civilizations and determine the level of their cultures. To do this, he makes use of a body of past experience, physical, written and pictorial, plus the necessary tools to dig up new finds. Some archeologists wonder if, in the historical evolution of civilization on Earth, it is possible that we have been the oblivious recipients of visitors from space who left behind little trace of their visits. They may have been here before our civilization began, or they may have left undisturbed the civilization they found because it was so far below their level that it had nothing to offer. History is dotted with unexplained phenomena which suggest that all of man's knowledge combined cannot account for some events.

Among the unexplained are a certain percentage of the so-called UFO (Unidentified Flying Objects) sightings, although the percentage is certainly negligible in relation to the number of claims. Better results might come from focussing attention on evidence that might be found on or in the Earth or out on the Moon or in our Solar System, that our part of the universe was once visited by explorations from space. To date there have been no such discoveries, but eventually we may find some evidence. As scientists explore the Solar System, then the Milky Way, they will certainly keep alert for signs of space visitors.

The astro-archeologist's task will be to help decipher any evidence of landings on other celestial bodies, because he better than anyone else will be able to discern whether or not a certain site has been used. He will be looking for

Featuring 50 to 100 people in artificial gravity, "trolley-track" vehicles to provide transport between modules, and multiple docking capability for Shuttle craft, this manned orbiting space station has been designed by Grumman.

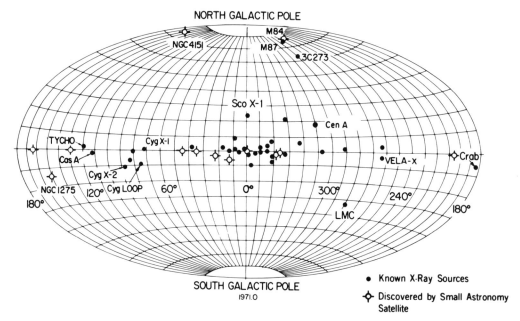

NORTH GALACTIC POLE

SOUTH GALACTIC POLE
1971.0

- Known X-Ray Sources
- ♦ Discovered by Small Astronomy Satellite

A new pulsating X-ray star, unlike any other known, was detected in 1971, in our Milky Way Galaxy by NASA's Explorer 42, a small astronomy satellite. The new pulsar, called Cygnus X-1, was found to be generating precisely-timed pulses every 15 seconds. Explorer 42 also discovered 13 new X-ray objects and confirmed the existence of a distant quasar.

indicators that "other beings" have left signs of their presence and perhaps intelligence. There may even be evidence of *how* they went about their explorations.

The archeologist, along with the anthropologist, the sociologist and the trained psychologist, will be needed on other celestial bodies to establish colonies. They can apply their knowledge of human activities and societies to the evolving cultures that are likely to develop on planetary outposts across the universe. In the long-distant future, the social scientists working on another planet may want to return to Earth to compare cultures. Such information could then be communicated to a long string of colonies that have been established.

By continuing to study the past on other celestial bodies, the archeologist and the anthropologist together may help us determine more exactly how our Earth and its civilization developed as part of the Solar System and the whole scheme of the Universe and the Cosmos.

What would happen if suddenly one of our lunar exploration teams sent back a message that they had found what seemed to be the remains of a long-vanished civilization in the region now known as Mare Tranquilitatis, on the Moon; or an abandoned site just outside the perimeter of what we call Amazonis on Mars? How would we go about interpreting such a discovery? What kind of interpretation would be needed if such a site were found on Titan, or Ganymede, or Jupiter? This is a matter for more than the astronaut who is an engineer, biologist, and communications expert—it would have to be left for investigation by an archeologist and an anthropologist.

Interplanetary Co-operation

Co-operation on Earth must come before co-operation in space. We could begin now to make the deserts bloom and the ice caps productive; to educate the more unfortunate peoples; to give everyone interested at least a knowledge (not simply an awareness) of basic astronomy and astrophysics; and to harness the great undeveloped resources on the Earth, if nations co-operated. Our only hope for improvement of our civilization is in a merging of the talents and abilities of the Family of Man.

The co-operative exploration of space, today as well as tomorrow, will depend upon a desire to get the job done, regardless of nationalism. Other

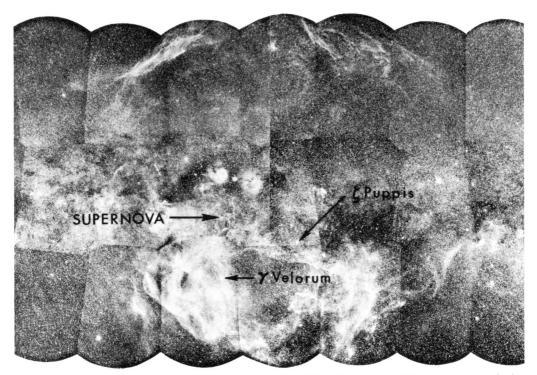

Composite of 21 separate photos taken by Mt. Stromolo Observatory of the Australian National University in Canberra shows the shell remnants of a supernova that produced the Gum Nebula. A supernova is a "new star" which flares up to many thousands of times its usual brightness in the sky, and then sinks in a few months or years back to its former obscurity, usually leaving remnants in the form of a nebula. About 60 per cent of the Gum Nebula, the brighter inner portion, is shown in this picture.

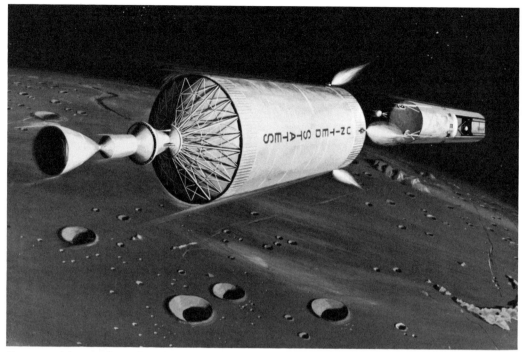

A re-usable nuclear Shuttle craft (left) proposed for deep space operations by North American Rockwell, is shown separating from a manned lunar surface payload it has placed into lunar orbit. The craft, powered by a nuclear engine, can be refueled in space for a multi-mission capability.

concepts are often better than our own, and we have to be ready to derive true satisfaction from the success of others and the success of combined efforts. The exploration of space will be best accomplished by astronauts, engineers, physicists, biologists, archeologists, sociologists, etc., whether American, Russian, German or any other nationality. We must marshal our energies and minds co-operatively. Space is filled with many awesome challenges. To pursue a course alone and recklessly, in a spirit of ill-defined self-interests, is to court certain disaster.

There is, fortunately, some light already at the end of this tunnel. The United States and Soviet governments and scientists have agreed to begin to co-operate in several ways. They have agreed to return each other's aborted or disabled spacecraft if they should fall on the other fellow's territory. They have also acknowledged that they will rescue and protect each others' downed astronauts, and their equipment, in a spirit of co-operation.

Each major American space expedition has delivered photographs and soil samples of the Moon to the Soviet Academy of Sciences. Even before this, the U.S. supplied Soviet scientists with pounds of photographs taken by Ranger, Surveyor, Orbiter and Mariner reconnaissance craft, and have given freely of the results of meteorological satellite investigations. In other words, there is now at least a mutually agreeable relationship where research is concerned. Soviet newsmen have been invited to every manned spacecraft launch of record.

Far more exciting than any of these agreements, however, is one in which U.S. and Soviet scientists have agreed to design and build standard rendezvous and docking assemblies on future spacecraft. In May, 1972, an agreement was made between the United States and the Soviet Union for a joint docking of manned spacecraft, scheduled for 1975. A United States Apollo spacecraft and a Soviet Soyuz spacecraft will latch together by way of two docking mechanisms—one on Apollo and one on Soyuz. The men from the Apollo spacecraft will then be able to pass into a specially constructed docking module corridor and airlock. The airlock will adjust the different atmospheres and pressures of the two spacecraft, after which the astronauts will continue into Soyuz and, thus, meet in space.

Perhaps the most gratifying example of such co-operation was portrayed in the recent motion picture film *Marooned in Space,* in which a Soviet Cosmonaut guided his spaceship out of orbit and sped to the aid of American astronauts disabled in space. The Cosmonaut was responsible for saving the American's life. Just a movie? True—but perhaps it's a story about to come true.

For years, NASA has entered into agreements with foreign countries (the co-operative German-American Helios launch is an excellent example) whereby U.S. aid is supplied to get foreign satellites into orbit. NASA has pursued a vigorous international space program in this regard, resulting in the launches of Ariel I, II and III (with the United Kingdom); Alouette I and II (with Canada); San Marco I and II (with Italy); several satellites with France, and a few with Australia. San Marco I was orbited by an American rocket from U.S. territory by an Italian firing crew; San Marco II was orbited by an American booster by an Italian crew from a floating platform off the East African coast. The satellite Wresat was launched by an American rocket from Australian territory, while the French Diamant rocket with U.S. help lifted the French satellites A-1, Diademe 1 and Diademe 2 into orbit.

As a brotherhood of concerned explorers, all astronauts will have a much better chance of exploring the universe; a group of self-interested adventurers can accomplish nothing. As bases are established on the Moon, on the planets, and much later on the planets of other solar systems in space, no one should be bothered with suspicions and fears of losing their national treasures. If the Russians place men on the Moon, what they discover can only help all plans to mount expeditions to the planets and stars. There will have to be stopping places in space, and all nations should help set them up. If a crisis should develop at some time, astronauts of all nations should feel obligated to help.

There is the matter of sharing expenses, too. Today it would seem to be asking a lot to have an international starship from *Earth*, designed, built and funded by several nations and manned by a crew of American, British, Soviet and German scientists. But science can have no limitations, and money or the lack of it should not stop scientific exploration.

The great popular triumph of Apollo 11 came about not so much because it included man's first step on the grainy soil of the Moon but because life throughout the world was momentarily suspended while people watched the mission on television. Those three astronauts went to the Moon ". . . in peace for all mankind," and all mankind watched in awed expectation, cheering them on. In New York, London, Tokyo, Seoul, Perth, Rome, Paris, Ottawa, Da Nang Airbase, Copenhagen, Johannesburg and hundreds of other places, people watched every move and held their breath at every critical moment. It will be the same when astronauts first land on Mars, or on Jupiter, or finally reach an unknown planet outside the Milky Way.

Perhaps economist James P. Warburg summed it up best when he wrote:

"We shall have to learn to think, not just as Americans, but as members of the human race—as peculiarly and uniquely fortunate members of the human race, endowed with an enormous potential for creative action. We shall have to learn to think, not in terms of charity or in terms of enlightened self-defense, but in terms of pioneers opening up new horizons, clearing new fields and conquering the desert areas. We shall have to shake off the corroding fear of losing what we possess and recapture the spirit of adventure, along with the affinity for all men everywhere seeking change for the better, which once made our nation a symbol of hope throughout the world."

This is an artist's vision of a complex orbiting space station, housing a population of 300 to 500 astronauts and scientists.

INDEX